ROSES
TREES
SHRUBS
VEGETABLES
HERBS
AND MUCH MORE . . .

It's all here in *A Garden of Your Own*—advice on designing, planting, nurturing, and enjoying your very own garden—whether you're just starting out or you want some tips for improving the garden you already have.

If you've always dreamed of growing a garden, let your dreams take root—with . . .

A GARDEN OF YOUR OWN

The Beginner's Guide to Growing Flowers, Vegetables, Herbs, Fruits, and More

A Garden of Your Own

Michael O'Brian

BERKLEY BOOKS, NEW YORK

A GARDEN OF YOUR OWN

A Berkley Book / published by arrangement with
Boldface Publishing

PRINTING HISTORY
Berkley edition / February 1993

ISBN: 0-425-13628-0

A BERKLEY BOOK ® ™ 757,375
Berkley Books are published by The Berkley Publishing Group,
200 Madison Avenue, New York, New York 10016.
The name "BERKLEY" and the "B" logo
are trademarks belonging to Berkley Publishing Corporation.

PRINTED IN THE UNITED STATES OF AMERICA

10   9   8   7   6   5   4   3   2   1

CONTENTS

1

1

GARDENING BASICS

PLANNING YOUR GARDEN

The first step in gardening is planning your garden. If you are starting from scratch, you need to plan the layout of your yard, deciding where you are going to put what plants. If you just bought a new house, you are going to decide what to do with every square foot of your yard. For most people, this means deciding where to put the trees and shrubs and flowers, and then planting grass everywhere else by default. But you don't have to have some kind of plant growing on every square inch of your property. Consider alternatives, such as brick walks, gravel paths, or plots of bark or stone surrounding trees or shrubs.

If you are inheriting someone else's garden, or if you have already done some gardening in your yard, you need to determine what to keep, what to change, and where to expand.

In either case, you don't have to do it all this spring. Particularly if your ideal plan involves a lot of work, consider doing it in steps, maybe over 2 or 3 years. This will also give you experience and knowledge about what grows well in your area, or even in different sections of your yard.

The first major factor to consider in planning a garden is the pattern of sunlight in various places in your yard. Watch to see what areas are sunny all day long, what sections get sun most or part of the day, and where there is little if any direct sunlight. Keep in mind that these patterns are going to shift as the days get longer in summer and start to get shorter again in the fall. Existing plants will give you an idea of what kinds of plants do well in your area in general as well as in various parts of your yard. Visit neighbors to see what kind of plants they have. If a particular shrub is growing well on the north side of a nearby house, odds are it will do well on the north side of your house.

Think about water, too, both getting water to an area and draining it away. If you have a sprinkler system, consider whether that will help or hurt flowers planted within its range. Make sure that plants that don't like a lot of water are planted in well-drained areas, not near a sidewalk or driveway, where water could be dammed up and form puddles.

In deciding on larger plants such as shrubs or trees, think about shade and privacy. A high hedge could give you a sheltered nook for sunbathing. A tree close to a window could shade out both the summer sun and the neighbor's view.

After you have decided what will actually grow in your yard, then you have to decide what you actually want to plant. The main reason for picking any particular plant is that it looks good in your yard. The second reason is that either it will look good inside the house, in the case of cut flowers, or that it will taste good, in the case of herbs or vegetables. Keep in mind that herbs and vegetables are usually not as attractive as flowers, so you may want to plant them in a back corner of the yard or behind some shrubs.

Here again, it's a good idea to check out the neighborhood in deciding what types of plants seem attractive with your type of house. Drive around, looking at houses of similar design, noting what plants look good and what plants don't. There's nothing wrong with stealing ideas from the neighbors or learning from their mistakes.

SOIL

Soil is a mixture of mineral particles, organic matter, water, and air. The primary characteristic of soil is its structure, or the size of its particles. The larger the soil particles, the more sandy the soil. (Carried to a further extreme, one could say that the coarsest soil is gravel.) Soil with relatively large particles is light, sandy, and doesn't hold water very well. Such soil also tends to be low in the nutrients needed by most plants, because nutrients are leached out by water draining quickly through it. The other end of the spectrum is soil with very small particles. This is clay, a very heavy soil that holds water very well. Although clay can have a lot of plant nutrients, its excessive wetness can cause root rot, and so heavy a soil can make it difficult for plant roots to spread.

The ideal soil is loam, which is roughly in the middle between clay and sand. Loam is spongy and can be compressed into small balls that break apart easily when pinched or tapped. Sand can't be squeezed into lumps or balls, while lumps of clay won't break apart easily. Loam holds moisture but drains excess water well. It also holds nutrients well.

Good soil is full of organic matter that decomposes into humus. Humus is partially decayed organic matter that conducts water and aerates the soil. It also has the basic nutrients needed by plants: nitrogen, phosphorus, and potassium. The best way to improve soil is to add organic matter. Adding organic matter to clay improves drainage and aerates the soil. Adding it to sandy soil improves the soil's ability to retain moisture and nutrients. Because organic matter in soil is constantly decaying, it needs to be replenished regularly. Organic matter needs nitrogen to decompose into humus. If nitrogen is not present in the organic matter itself, it is taken from the soil and is not available for the plants.

Peat moss and manure have plenty of nitrogen naturally. Straw, bark, and raw wood products need added nitrogen to aid in the decomposition process. There are three major sources of organic matter: animal manure, plant humus, and tilled-under cover crops.

Animal manure should be old and well rotted. Steer manure is best, and can be purchased in sacks at nurseries, hardware stores, or supermarkets. Work it well into the soil, breaking up the clods of dirt. While manure is very high in nutrients, it is not as good as plant humus for lightening heavy soil such as clay.

The second method is to add plant humus, such as peat moss. Peat moss is lower in nutrients than steer manure, but is better at lightening heavy clay soil. For best results, moisten the peat moss first before working it into the soil. If your soil is heavy clay, a good compromise is to add a combination of manure for nutrients and peat moss for texture.

The third method, which is really practical only for very large gardens, is to plant cover crops, such as clover or rye, and till them under. This is a small version of the farming practice of crop rotation.

Soil can also be improved by using compost. You can make a compost heap by alternating layers of organic material (leaves, kitchen scraps, etc.) and soil. Heap it in a pile or use some kind of container such as a wire bin, an old oil drum, a box made of concrete blocks, or just about anything. Keep the pile moist and turn it occasionally to speed decomposition. The compost is ready when the organic matter is broken down into very small pieces. Use it fairly coarse for mulch, finer for seedlings or potting.

FERTILIZER

Nutrients can be added directly to the soil through the use of fertilizer. Fertilizers can be organic, from animal or vegetable matter, or inorganic, made from petrochemicals. Inorganic fertilizers are usually cheaper, quicker, and easier to use, but overuse of these chemicals can kill beneficial soil organisms.

Commercial fertilizers use a standard formula to tell what nutrients are in the product. The basic plant nutrients are nitrogen (chemical symbol N), phosphorus (P), and potassium (K). Commercial fertilizer packages have three numbers on the front, in the format N-P-K, giving the percentage of each nutrient contained in the mix. If a package says "20-10-5" on the label, it contains 20% nitrogen, 10% phosphorus, 5% potassium, and 65% inert ingredients.

Nitrogen is not a mineral, and therefore is not naturally present in soil. It can only get into the soil from organic matter or from fertilizer. While potassium and phosphorus are naturally present in soil, it is difficult for plants to acquire and use these nutrients. The plant root must actually come in contact with these minerals in order to pick them up. Therefore the best and most efficient way to ensure that your plants are getting sufficient nutrients is to use fertilizer.

The average garden will do well with a single, commercial, complete and balanced fertilizer. Complete means that it contains significant amounts of all three major nutrients. Balanced means that the percentage of each nutrient is roughly the same. A 10-10-10 mix is perfectly balanced. Any fertilizer is considered balanced if no number is more than twice as large as any other. A few plants do not tolerate large doses of a particular nutrient, such as nitrogen. Avoid feeding such a plant with a rich, balanced fertilizer.

Commercial fertilizers come in two forms: dry and liquid. Dry fertilizers can be powder, granular, or solid. They are designed to be spread over the surface of the ground (sometimes called top feeding or top dressing) or to be mixed into the soil before planting. Dry fertilizers usually last longer per application than liquids.

Liquid fertilizers usually come in concentrated form and need to be mixed with water before using. Be sure to read the package directions carefully before applying. Liquids are generally easier to use than dry fertilizers and are less likely to damage (burn) the plant if used properly. Liquids tend to be more costly than dry fertilizers and generally must be reapplied more frequently.

Nutrients are also available from organic sources. Steer manure is a good source of nitrogen, although the soil should also be lightened with peat moss. Bone meal is high in phosphorus, and wood ash or leaf compost is rich in potassium. Different plants do better on different types of nutrients. Particularly when starting young plants, check to see what nutrients they need, and provide them through soil additives. Organic or natural fertilizers tend to be unbalanced and are often incomplete, missing one or even two of the basic nutrients. For example, bone meal has an average analysis of 2.5–24–0, while wood ash is 0–2–5. If you use organic fertilizers, you will generally have to use 2 or more to get a good balance of nutrients.

The term *organic* means that the nutrients come from the remains of a once-living organism, whether plant or animal. There is no evidence that organic fertilizers do any better job of feeding plants than the chemical varieties. Chemical fertilizers are usually cheaper and easier to use. Excess use of any fertilizer, whether chemical or organic, will damage or kill plants.

SUNLIGHT

Most commercially available seedlings or seed packages have some information about the amount of sunlight the particular plant requires or likes. This is a general indication. Actual light requirements are also affected by other factors such as climate, soil, and water. Here, as elsewhere, experience is the best teacher. If the growing plant is relatively short with few leaves, it is probably not getting enough light. Alternatively, a plant not getting enough light may have relatively few but exceptionally long shoots in an attempt to reach out for more light. If a plant is getting too much sunlight, its leaves will be wilted and scorched.

The following are general guidelines for common terminology:

Full Sun: 6 or more hours a day, particularly during the period from 10 A.M. to 6 P.M. This includes most fruits and vegetables as well as most flowers. Plants like tomatoes or sunflowers require even more sunlight.

Light Sun or Part Shade: shade during the most intensely sunny part of the day. Plants in this category like the dappled shade of a tree or under lath structures.

Bright Shade: under a full tree or next to a house wall.

Full Shade: no direct sunlight. For plants such as ferns or rhododendrons.

WATER

Water's basic function is to move nutrients through the plant, as well as providing firmness to many parts of the plant. Insufficient water results in an undernourished plant that wilts and eventually dies. Too much water is just as bad, robbing the plant of oxygen and leading to rot and death. Excess water can also transmit plant diseases.

Water requirements vary with the type of plant and with location. Plants with shallow root systems need more water, and need it more frequently. More deeply rooted plants should be watered less frequently, encouraging the roots to grow deep to find water. If these plants are not watered deeply, the roots will grow too shallow, subjecting the plant to damage when it does not get enough water. Plants should be watered to the width and depth of their root systems. Shady areas dry more slowly, while sun, wind, and heat cause quicker drying and the need for more water. Plants should be watered more frequently when the weather is hot and dry, less frequently when it is cool and humid. You also need to consider the type of soil in your garden. Sandy soil has poor water retention and needs more frequent watering. Clay, on the other hand, holds water very well and drains poorly. Make sure to avoid overwatering if your soil contains a lot of clay.

The terrain of your garden also affects watering. If you have steep slopes, the ground will be prone toward water runoff and erosion. Avoid these problems by terracing steep slopes—by building walls of stone, brick, or timbers. Also keep an eye out for poor drainage, especially puddles. Channel water away from such spots, making sure that the drainage is good.

Keep the soil around new plants (except bulbs) moist but not overly damp. Try to water deeply to encourage deep root growth. Where possible, try to water below the leaves of plants. Wet leaves can lead to sunburn and the growth of disease organisms.

Sprinklers work well in getting water to a large area. The disadvantage is that a lot of the water is lost to evaporation, and sprinklers get water on the leaves and flowers, which can harm certain plants, especially in full sunlight. Flooding or soaking is a good way to get water to the deep roots of trees and shrubs. Make a basin around the tree trunk with a ridge of dirt. Slowly fill the basin with water and let it soak into the ground. The same thing can be done with furrows between rows of plants.

You can also water deeply with a soaker hose. This special hose is made of canvas or porous plastic. It is attached to the garden hose and laid along the ground next to the plants or in a circle around a tree trunk. Water seeps out along the entire length of the hose.

Tree and shrub roots can also be deep-watered with a root irrigator. This is a long, thin, hollow metal rod with a hose connection. It is pushed into the ground for its full 2-to-3-foot length. Water then flows out the tip below the ground.

CLIMATE

The United States Department of Agriculture (USDA) has developed a system whereby the country is divided into winter hardiness zones based on average minimum winter temperatures. These ratings are used on many seed packages as an indication of where in the country a particular flower will grow and when it should be planted.

Keep in mind that these zones or ratings are very broad estimates. They do not and cannot take into consideration local conditions such as maximum temperatures, dryness or wetness of a particular area, local light and soil conditions, and so on. Also, remember that even within a relatively small area, microclimates are possible. These climate variations within a short distance can be caused by prevailing winds, proximity to water, the differences between a windy hill and a protected valley, and so on.

The USDA winter hardiness zones are useful, but need to be tempered by experience in growing plants in your area.

EQUIPMENT

You could plant a garden using some kitchen utensils and a few pots, but you wouldn't want to, any more than you would want to drive a nail using a shoe or a brick. The proper tools make the job a lot easier and a lot less trouble.

The first thing you will notice when shopping for garden tools is that there are any number of similar-looking tools at a wide range of prices. In general, the more expensive a trowel or a spade, the better the materials that went into it, the better the workmanship, the better the job it will do, the easier it will be to work with, and the longer it will last.

Most garden tools are made up of two parts: the metal working end and the wooden handle. The metal part of the tool should be one piece of metal, with the wooden handle firmly attached, preferably with a metal rivet completely through the tool.

Look at the thickness (gauge) of the metal: the thicker the better. Check the metal part to see if it says that the tool was forged, which is better than stamped, and if it is heat-treated or tempered, which is better than not. If it doesn't say anything, ask the store clerk.

The best wood for tool handles is ash. It is strong and durable. This is what baseball bats are made from. As an indication of quality, see if the grain in the handle is straight, and that there are no knots in the wood.

The most basic gardening chore is digging. This includes preparing the soil and making holes for the individual plants.

At a minimum, you will need a garden trowel. This is a small, one-handed, pointed digging tool that looks something like a foot-long shovel. A trowel is useful for digging smaller holes and for digging up seedlings and other plants for transplanting. Find one that feels comfortable in your hand. You may want to get a couple, one small and one large, for different jobs.

For more extensive digging, and for tilling and preparing garden beds, a spade is a very handy tool. A spade is a small shovel with a relatively flat blade. The blade on a gardening spade is usually rectangular rather than sharp or pointed. Sometimes called a flat-point spade, this tool is very handy for tilling soil, edging, digging holes for trees and shrubs, and digging up shrubs for transplanting. A good tool for extensive soil preparation is a spading fork. This is smaller and stouter than a pitchfork, with four flat tines used for turning and loosening soil.

If you have a big garden and move a lot of material around, you may want to get a round-point shovel or even a scoop shovel. The latter is good for moving bulky but light material such as compost. A pitchfork works well for some mulch such as hay or straw.

At a minimum, you'll need a small hand weeding tool to make it easy to dig weeds out by the roots. For a bigger garden, a hoe can be used to weed, to do shallow soil preparation, and to break up dirt clods.

Depending on your needs, you will probably need various tools for cutting and clipping. These can include a pruning knife, a hand pruner, hedge trimmers, or even a pruning saw.

Finally, you will need a way to water your garden. A watering can makes watering pots or small plots easy, without all the bother of unwinding a hose, dragging it around, and hanging it back up again. But it is pretty hard to get along without a hose, along with one or more nozzles. Large areas can be watered easily and quickly with a sprinkler, but this has the disadvantage of getting leaves and flowers wet as well as losing a lot of water through evaporation. Remember that the best way to water most plants is with a gentle shower of water under the leaves. Some kind of adjustable nozzle works well, or try one of the watering tools that looks like a shower head at the end of a long metal tube. These allow you to get the water source down under the plant leaves. A soaker hose is also a good way to water deeply without getting leaves or flowers wet.

BUYING PLANTS

The best place to buy plants is at a nursery, and the best plants to buy at any particular nursery are the ones that they have grown themselves. Talk to the people who work there. If they can't answer your questions, or don't seem sure of themselves, talk to the owners. In a small nursery, all of the staff should be knowledgeable, although they may specialize in certain kinds of plants. Larger nurseries may have seasonal help who are just learning the business. Don't be afraid to ask around until you feel confident that the information you are getting is right.

Many supermarkets and discount stores sell plants. You can get good plants here, and get a good deal on them, if you stick to plants you know about and make sure that the ones you buy are in good condition. If you need help or information, skip the supermarket and stick to a good nursery.

The secret of buying a healthy plant is knowing what to avoid. Don't buy plants with yellowed or wilted leaves. These could be okay, but why take a chance. Avoid tall, spindly plants. Look for a plant with bushy, compact leaves and a relatively large number of stems. Also avoid plants in bloom. The flowers look pretty, but the plant will grow better if it flowers in your garden and not in the supermarket. Check the root system. A plant with an underdeveloped root system will come out of the pot with little effort. Potbound plants have roots curling and crawling out of the pot. Avoid both extremes.

PLANTING

The best way to prepare soil for gardening is to till it by hand, using a spade or a spading fork. Remove weeds and rocks as you go, and work manure, peat moss, or whatever else you decide on into the soil at the same time. The depth to which you till depends on the plants. Grass needs about 6 inches of prepared soil, while deep-rooted perennials need about 2 feet.

It is traditional to plant in rows, particularly when planting large plots. There are reasons for this. One is that plants need a certain amount of uncontested space for their root systems, without encroachment by the roots of other plants, particularly weeds. Planting in rows gives enough room between the rows for the plants, and allows later thinning along the rows as the plants develop. Also, planting in rows allows space to walk between the plants to tend them and to pull weeds, as well as providing a clear distinction between where the plants were placed and where weeds are growing.

It is very important to avoid planting outdoors too early, particularly in the cooler climates. Seeds, or even seedlings, placed in cold damp ground too early will rot and die. If there is any doubt about frost, especially with less hardy plants, either wait or start them indoors. Take care in planting, or even in tilling soil, in the early part of the season. Raised beds, formed by mounding up soil, drain more quickly and warm up sooner than level soil. You can also warm a plot by covering it with a sheet of plastic, although this can retain moisture, defeating the purpose. Cultivation will also warm the soil sooner, exposing it to the sun and air. But be careful not to till the soil while it is still very damp, or you run the risk of packing it down. Never use a power tiller on wet soil. The soil can be damaged for years.

When to plant varies greatly from one plant to another. Some can tolerate late frost or cold ground or wet soil, while others will quickly die. Some specific information is given in the discussion of individual plants later in this book, but in general you should not plant before the soil is easily workable, and you should wait until after the average date for the last frost in your area. Soil is workable when you roll a handful into a ball and it breaks up easily when you poke it with your finger.

Plants can be started new or planted as seedlings. Starting new plants is done by planting seeds or by planting divisions or cuttings of existing plants. Sowing seeds directly into the garden has the advantage of avoiding transplanting, which is a shock to the young plant. You may also grow plants from seed by starting them indoors in pots to avoid bad weather in late spring.

Seeds for some flowers, particularly wildflowers, can just be spread or scattered onto bare earth or into prepared earth in the areas that you want flowers. Other seeds require a little more care in planting, including careful soil preparation and fertilization. You may want to plant some flowers or vegetables in rows, both for looks and for easier weeding, pruning, and watering. Plants grown from seeds generally require some thinning after they have come up. Check the specific reference later in the book to see how much a given type of plant should be thinned.

You can start seedlings indoors in many different types of containers. The containers should be easy to handle and have good drainage. Thoroughly clean out any containers that have been used for plants before. You can use prepared potting soil or just dig up some soil from your own garden. Prepared soil is disease free and contains organic matter. Soil from your own garden should be sterilized by baking in the oven for a couple of hours at about 170 degrees. This will kill any harmful organisms. Garden soil also has the advantage of being the same soil that the seedling will be transplanted to eventually.

Transplant seedlings into the garden when they have developed their second set of leaves, assuming that the weather is mild enough for the particular plant. If there is still a danger of a harmful frost, you may have to thin out the seedlings in place and wait for better weather. Thinned-out plants can be transplanted into other containers awaiting planting in the garden.

Perennials, bulbs, tubers, and rhizomes are propagated by division. Every 2 to 4 years, the root clump grows too large for its space and the growth of the plant itself suffers. The solution is to dig up the root clump, divide it into 2 or more parts, and replant the divisions. Each will form a new healthy plant. Division is best done when the plant is dormant, in fall or early spring. Division in many plants is best accomplished by dividing off the young outer growth and discarding the older core. Check the particular sections of this book dealing with individual plants for specifics.

Most gardeners plant from seedlings rather than from seeds. Seedlings are generally in small plastic packs of 4 or 6 plants, or in individual peat pots or small plastic pots. Make sure that these seedlings do not dry out while waiting to be planted.

To set out a seedling, first dig a hole just larger than the root ball. Turn the seedling container upside down and tap the seedling out into your hand. Remove seedlings from plastic packs by pushing up against the bottom of the pack with your thumb, lifting the root ball with your fingers. Plants in individual pots can be removed by placing your hand over the top of the pot and turning it upside down. The plant should slide right out with minimal tapping or shaking. Plants in peat pots should be planted pot and all, making sure that the pot is moist before planting. Also make sure that all of the peat pot is below ground, or the pot will wick moisture away from the plant.

After removing the seedling, if there is a mat of tangled roots at the bottom of the ball of soil, tear it off. Loosen the roots by pulling apart the bottom third of the root ball. Place the seedling in a hole just deep enough so that the top of the root ball is at ground level. Holding it by the root ball, and not by the stem, place it in the hole and press down to make sure that no air is trapped around the root ball. Fill the hole with loosely packed soil and water with a liquid fertilizer designed for starting seedlings.

When setting out seedlings, or when thinning out plants sown directly into the garden, remember that each plant has its own space requirements. Plants located too close together will compete for space and nutrients, and both will suffer. Seedlings are best set out on a cloudy day or in late afternoon for maximum protection from the full heat of the sun after the shock of being transplanted. Water the seedling with fertilizer dissolved in water. Use a starter fertilizer high in phosphorus, such as a 15–30–15 formula.

Many perennials are sold as dormant, bare-root plants. They are packed in a loose damp material such as sawdust. Keep them moist until planting. Plant in a hole with a cone of dirt in the center. Drape the roots over the cone, taking care that the plant is at the proper depth, which differs from plant to plant. Fill the hole with soil and water.

Trees and shrubs are generally sold bare-root when dormant. At other times, they will be either balled and burlapped or in a container, such as a large fiber pot or a plastic pot. Bare-root trees or shrubs should be planted like the perennials discussed above, with a cone of dirt in the center of a hole.

Potted plants can usually be easily removed by inverting the pot and tapping it a few times. With fiber pots, it may be easier to cut away the pot with a large knife. Place in a hole so that the soil line of the plant is a few inches above the ground level. Cut off any kinked roots. Spread the roots out in the hole, fill in with soil, and water thoroughly. Make a ridge of dirt around the plant to form a watering basin.

Balled and burlapped plants are dug up with a ball of soil around the root system and wrapped in burlap or some other material. Such plants should be lifted and carried only by the ball, never using the tree trunk as a handle. To plant, dig a hole twice as wide as the root ball. Place the plant in the hole. If the root ball is wrapped in burlap or some other biodegradable material, you can just untie it and pull the material down to expose the upper half of the root ball. If synthetic material is used, it will have to be removed. Fill the hole about halfway with soil, adding some organic matter. If you are planting in a windy site, the new plant should be staked. Drive a stake firmly into the ground on the side of the plant toward the prevailing winds. Then finish filling the hole with soil and water well. Tie the plant to the stake and form a watering basin around the plant with a ridge of soil. Keep the ground around the new plant moist but not soggy.

MULCH

Mulch is a ground cover placed around plants to hold in moisture and hold down weeds. It also prevents soil erosion, warms the ground, and in some cases enriches the soil. Mulch is a generic term for anything that can do these things, and can include bark, leaves, peat moss, sheets of plastic, or most anything else. The important things are that the mulch does the job and that it is inexpensive. What you use will depend on what is readily and cheaply available in your area. Sawmill products such as bark, sawdust, or wood chips work well, as do leaves, grass clippings, and pine needles. Hay or straw can also be used. Plastic is also widely used, particularly in the north, where clear plastic lets the sunlight through, warming the soil and lengthening the growing season. You can also buy a black plastic sheeting specifically designed for mulch. It has a network of tiny holes in it that let water soak in, but it keeps weeds from growing up under it.

PRUNING

Pruning is done to modify the way the plant is growing. It is done to remove dead or diseased wood, to direct growth, or to encourage growth of flowers or fruit.

Plant growth takes place at the bud. A stem or a branch has a terminal bud at the end and lateral buds along the sides. The stem or branch grows longer through the growth at the terminal bud. The lateral buds produce the sideways growth that makes a plant bushy. If the terminal bud is pruned or cut off, growth will be redirected toward another bud lower on the stem. Therefore, all pruning should be done just above a bud. That bud will then be the focus of growth for that branch or stem.

The simplest form of pruning is pinching back a new

plant. Pinching back the main stem on a new plant will encourage growth at the other buds, making it bushier than it would have been. If you want a plant to grow tall, pinch back lateral buds to encourage growth at the terminal bud.

Cutting back is a more drastic form of pinching. This involves cutting off well-developed lengths of stems to encourage growth of other, perhaps less-developed stems or to encourage new growth. Cutting flowers is an example of cutting back, which gives you flowers for the house and encourages new growth in the garden.

In any kind of pruning, always make the cut just above some form of growth, whether a bud or a stem or a branch. Cut at a 45-degree angle, with the lower part of the cut opposite the bud or stem.

2

ANNUALS

Annuals are plants that complete their life cycles in a single growing season. An annual starts off as a seed in the spring, flowers, produces seeds, and dies the same year. Annuals grow and mature quickly, producing an abundance of flowers. Annuals are a very good source of cut flowers, since they produce even more blooms if they are cut. In an appropriate climate and soil, the seeds an annual drops during the year will sprout in the following spring. But in most cases, they will have to be reseeded or planted from seedlings.

Annuals have fairly small root systems. Therefore they require relatively little space in the garden, and they can be transplanted easily if necessary. This also means that they are well suited to growing in pots, where they can be moved around easily for variety, for proper sun, and for protection against wind and heavy rain.

There are several types of annuals, classified basically according to how sturdy they are. Warm-weather annuals grow and bloom best during warm weather. These include zinnia and lobelia. Cool-weather annuals include bachelor button or African violet. These plants cannot take extreme heat.

Annuals can be further classified as tender, half-hardy, or hardy. Any of these types may be either warm- or cool-weather annuals. Tender annuals cannot endure frost. These include zinnia and marigolds. They cannot be sown or set out until all danger of frost is past.

Half-hardy annuals, such as petunias, can take a minimal exposure to frost, but not as much as hardy annuals. Hardy annuals can take some frost. They can be sown or planted in early spring, as soon as the ground can be worked. Most annuals require full sunlight, except in the very hottest climates, and plenty of water.

PLANTING ANNUALS

The most important factor in planting annuals is coordinating the planting time with the last expected frost and the particular plant's tolerance for frost. Seed packets will give you information about the plant's ability to survive frost. If in doubt, start seedlings indoors and replant outside when you feel it is safe. The alternative is to buy seedlings from a nursery in middle-to-late spring and set them out. Nursery seedlings are relatively inexpensive, unless you are planting a lot of flowers.

Annuals are shallow-rooted and do not require deep prepared soil. The soil should not be too wet when planting. The ideal condition is when a handful of soil can be compressed easily into a ball, and the ball of soil will crumble when flicked with a finger. Annuals prefer a richer soil than perennials, but take care to avoid excessive nitrogen, which tends to produce more leaves and fewer flowers. Use a balanced fertilizer, such as a 5–10–5 mixture, working it into the hole before transplanting. Feed a few weeks later with liquid fertilizer.

If planting early in the spring, annual seeds should be planted fairly shallowly, about ⅛ to ¼ inch, to ensure the full effect of the sun's warmth. Later in the season, plant seeds about ½ inch deep to protect against heat and drying. Properly spacing the seeds can be tricky. Larger seeds can be held in the palm of the hand and planted one at a time. Medium-size seeds should be gently tapped or shaken out of the seed packet, a few at a time. Very small seeds can be mixed with fine sand or coarse soil and sprinkled onto the ground.

Make sure that young plants are planted where they get sufficient sun, at least 6 hours a day. Avoid planting annuals close to tree roots, or where there is poor drainage. Annuals require more water than perennials. Make sure that they don't dry out.

Pinching off the ends of young plants will cause them to branch out and become bushier. This should be done early in the season, when plants are 4 to 6 inches tall. Plants that respond well to pinching include petunias and snapdragons, as well as such perennials as asters and chrysanthemums. Pinching back the plant early encourages it to grow husky and bushy. It will then be in better shape later in the season when it begins to blossom. In buying seedlings, look for a husky, bushy plant with dark leaves and sturdy side branches, ignoring whether or not it has any blossoms.

As mentioned above, picking or cutting flowers also encourages them to grow. Pull off dead blooms too, unless you want them to self-seed. Many annuals can also be dug up before first frost, potted, and brought inside. Some, such as impatiens or geraniums, should last all winter indoors.

COMMON AND POPULAR ANNUALS

AGERATUM: Fuzzy flowers, sometimes growing up to 2 feet high. Flowers are usually blue or violet, but some are pink or white. These are tender, warm-weather plants, but they can do well in cooler climates if started indoors. They should be started indoors about 6 weeks before the last expected frost, then set out. Plant close together in full sun and rich moist soil, pinching back once to encourage growth. In very hot climates, they will do better in partial shade.

ALTHAEA: Also known as hollyhock, these plants grow 4 to 6 feet tall and produce large flowers up to 4 to 6 inches across. They were originally biennials, flowering only in their second year. Annual hollyhocks flower in the first year, and may bloom a second year as well. They do best in full sun and require average soil. Sow indoors about 6 weeks before the last frost. When the first leaves appear, transplant into small individual pots. When the weather is warm (above 50 degrees at night) set them out about 18 inches apart.

ALYSSUM: A hardy annual with tiny flowers growing in clumps, usually no more than 6 inches tall. Generally white, but sometimes pink or purple. Sow seeds directly in garden in early spring. They prefer cooler weather, and do best in full sun, but they can tolerate partial shade.

BABY'S BREATH: The plant grows to about 18 inches tall, producing a profusion of tiny blossoms, usually white. They only flower for about 6 weeks, so they are better as a source of cut flowers than as a garden plant. Sow directly in the garden after the last frost, spacing the plants about 12 inches apart. For a constant supply of flowers, resow every 3 to 4 weeks. They prefer full sun and do best in soil that is not too rich in nutrients.

BACHELOR BUTTON: A hardy annual that grows 2 to 3 feet tall. Bachelor buttons produce wide, ragged flowers that are usually blue. These are cool-weather plants that can be sown in early spring. Plant in full sun, in light soil that is not too acidic. Add lime to the soil to reduce acidity if necessary.

BEGONIA: See **WAX BEGONIA**

CALENDULA: Calendula produces yellow and orange flowers that look like daisies. Sow in early spring in cooler climates, in late summer or early fall in warmer areas. Plant about 1 ½ inches deep and about 12 inches apart. They prefer cool weather and full sun. Remove dead flowers to encourage blooming.

CLEOME: A half-hardy annual with large pink or white blossoms. The plants grow 3 to 5 feet high and are very fragrant. A warm-weather plant, it will flower in late summer to early fall. Start indoors and set out after all frost danger has passed. Cleome does best in full sun with good drainage.

COLEUS: Coleus is a tender plant growing about 1 to 3 feet high. It has very distinct markings and color patterns in leaves. It is best to buy started plants. Set out the seedlings after all danger of frost has passed. It is a warm-weather plant, but prefers part shade in very hot climates. In ideal conditions, it is actually a perennial.

CORNFLOWER: Cornflowers produce 2-inch ragged blossoms, usually blue, on a 2 to 3 foot stalk. Sow them directly in the garden in the early fall so that they begin to grow before first frost, or in spring as soon as the soil can be worked. Plant about 12 inches apart.

COSMOS: A half-hardy annual, growing from 2 to 8 feet tall with daisylike flowers, usually pink or red. Sow outdoors after last frost in full sun or very light partial shade. Pinch back once to encourage blooms.

DAHLIA: Dahlias are tender perennials from Mexico, usually grown as annuals in northern climates. They usually grow 1 to 2 feet high, although wild species can reach 15 to 20 feet in height. The types grown as annuals are early-flowering dwarfs grown from seed. Dahlias do best in full sun and rich, well-drained soil. Sow indoors about 8 weeks before the last frost and set out the seedlings about 12 inches apart after the last frost. Keep the soil around the plants slightly moist, particularly during hot weather.

DIANTHUS: There are over 300 species of dianthus, with many that are grown as annuals and others grown as perennials. The family includes annual varieties of pinks, carnations, and sweet william. Smaller varieties are used as edging plants, while larger varieties can grow up to 2 feet high with blossoms up to 3 inches across.

They grow best in full sun and well-drained alkaline soil. Add lime to acidic soil to neutralize it. Sow pinks and carnations indoors about 8 weeks before the last frost, moving the seedlings to a cold frame after about a month. After the last frost, set them out about 8 inches apart. Pinch back all but the top bud on each carnation stem for large showy flowers. Sweet william can be sown directly outdoors as soon as the soil can be worked.

FORGET-ME-NOT: Hardy, about a foot tall, usually bright blue flowers. Actually a biennial, they can be sown in the fall to bloom in spring and early summer. Or start indoors in late winter and set out in early spring. They prefer moist soil in light shade.

GERANIUM: A perennial grown as an annual in northern climates, geraniums have large red, pink, or white flower clusters. Start indoors early, or dig up and pot in the fall and keep inside over the winter. They prefer full sun, but can tolerate partial shade. Take care to avoid intense heat, and keep them well watered.

HELIOTROPE: Heliotropes are perennials in their native Peru, but are grown as annuals in the north. Plants grow to 1 to 2 feet high, with large flower clusters up to a foot in diameter. Most flowers are heliotrope blue, but some are white or purple, with a very distinctive aroma. They do best in full sun and rich soil, although potted heliotropes prefer partial shade, particularly during the hottest part of the day. Heliotrope is best grown from seedlings, planted in the spring about a foot apart.

HIBISCUS: Hibiscus range widely in size, from flower-of-an-hour, with 1-inch blossoms on a 2-foot plant, to sunset hibiscus, which grows up to 9 feet tall with flowers up to 9 inches across. The individual blossoms do not last long, but the plant flowers from midsummer until late fall. The blossoms die quickly after being cut. They do best in rich soil and full sun.

Sunset hibiscus should be started indoors about 8 weeks before the last frost in small peat pots. Set out after the last frost about 18 inches apart. Flower-of-an-hour should be sown directly in the garden after the last frost, with about a foot between the plants.

IMPATIENS: Tender annuals that grow well in partial shade, but can tolerate full sun. Impatiens prefer rich, moist soil. Some varieties are perennials, particularly in warmer climates. They usually grow about a foot high in a wide variety of colors. They can cover a wide area. It is best to start impatiens indoors 6 to 7 weeks before last frost, or to buy flats from the nursery. They are warm-weather plants and cannot stand any frost. Pinch the plants back to make them more compact and bushy.

LANTANA: A half-hardy annual that can grow very tall, particularly in warm climates. In very warm areas, lantana grows as an evergreen, flowering year around. It produces small clusters of red, pink, and orange flowers. These are warm-weather plants, best sown indoors in late winter. They do best in full sun, and care should be taken to avoid excessive watering or feeding.

LARKSPUR: Larkspur produces flowery spikes much like delphiniums, growing about 2 to 4 feet high. Sow directly in the garden in early spring in the north, late summer to early fall in the south. Larkspur prefers full sun except in very hot climates, where partial shade is better. It blooms in cooler weather in spring or early summer.

LOBELIA: A hardy annual, lobelia grows 6 to 8 inches tall, usually with blue flowers about ½ inch across. Some varieties are perennials. It does well as an edging plant or in hanging baskets or window boxes. Sow indoors about 10 to 12 weeks before the last frost. Sow the seeds directly on top of the soil without covering. Plant the seedlings 6 inches apart, in full sun in cooler areas, partial shade in hot climates. Lobelia does best with rich soil and constant moisture through the growing season.

MARIGOLD: A half-hardy annual with many varieties, with wide ranges in size and color, especially white, yellow, and orange. Some varieties are perennials in hot climates. Sow outdoors around the time of the last frost. Marigolds prefer full sun except in very hot climates. Water well and pick off dead blooms to encourage growth.

MOONFLOWER: Moonflowers grow on twining vines with large heart-shaped leaves and white blossoms up to 6 inches across. The flowers usually open at sunset and close before noon the next day. They will grow up to 10 feet high in a single year. They are perennials in the tropics, but are grown as annuals in the north. They require full sun, but do well in average soil. Soak the seeds overnight, and sow in individual pots about 8 weeks before the last frost. Set out in warm weather (nights above 50 degrees) about a foot apart with string or trellis support.

MORNING GLORY: There are more than 200 species of morning glory. The flowers usually open only from dawn until midmorning, with blossoms up to 8 inches across. Newer varieties stay open most of the day, particularly in cloudy weather. The plant is a vine, reaching up to 10 feet high after a few months. They prefer full sun, and soil that is not too rich or moist. Sow the seeds directly in the garden after the last frost, planting about ½ inch deep and 12 inches apart. Provide string or trellis support.

NASTURTIUM: A tender annual with 2-inch flowers in a wide range of colors, it grows as a perennial in warmer climates. Nasturtiums grow rapidly and are easy to care for. Stems are long and breakable. Sow around the time of the last frost. They prefer full sun and sandy soil. They need very good drainage, and don't require a lot of water. Avoid overfertilizing. Nasturtiums normally don't require feeding. They are very good for cut flowers.

PANSY: Actually a short-lived perennial that is grown as an annual. Many hybrids, with bicolored or tricolored flowers. Sow indoors about 10 weeks before last frost. Set out in spring in moist soil. Pansies don't like excess heat. Pick often to increase blooms.

PETUNIA: Petunias are a tender perennial usually grown as half-hardy annuals. They bloom in many colors, with flowers up to 4 inches across. They grow 6 to 18 inches high, depending on variety. Sow the seeds indoors about 9 weeks before the average last frost in moist sphagnum moss on top of soil-filled pots. Drop the seeds in the moss, and don't cover with soil. When the seedlings have produced 3 to 4 leaves, transplant them to individual small pots. Set out the seedlings about 12 inches apart after the last frost. Petunias are warm-weather plants, but may not like excessive heat. If straggly, cut back. Feed monthly with a balanced fertilizer. They do best in full sun, good soil, and require regular watering. After the plants are well established, cut them back by about a half to encourage growth.

Traditionally, petunias were of two types: singles or doubles. Singles have funnel-shaped flowers with open throats. Doubles have heavy ruffles and multipetal flowers. Newer varieties are hybrids that are more uniform in size and color, and are hardier than ordinary petunias.

PHLOX: Annual phlox originated as a wildflower in Texas, and grows best in very hot climates. Dwarf plants grow up to 8 inches tall with flowers about an inch across. Taller varieties grow up to 18 inches tall. The dwarf variety makes a good edging or border plant. They do best in well-drained soil. Sow directly in the garden after the last frost, spacing the plants about 6 inches apart. Cut back straggly plants to about 2 inches above the ground to encourage new growth and flowers.

PORTULACA: Tender annuals with needlelike leaves and brilliant flowers from early summer until first frost. Very drought resistant. Difficult to transplant. Start directly in the garden when the weather is warm. Portulaca requires full sun and good drainage, and does best in slightly sandy soil.

SILVIA: These plants produce blue spike flowers 2 to 3 feet tall. It is best to buy seedlings; seeds take a long time to flower. Transplant when the danger of frost is past. They prefer warm weather and require frequent watering.

SNAPDRAGON: Snapdragons are actually a perennial, but they are usually grown as an annual. They have tall spikes, growing up to 4 feet high, with red, pink, purple, orange, or white flowers. Sow them indoors about 6 weeks before the last frost, or buy flats from your nursery, and set out in the early fall in the south, in the spring in the north. Pinch them back when they are about 5 inches high for more blooms. Avoid overhead watering.

SWEET PEA: Most sweet peas are climbers, growing up to 10 feet high with 1-to-2-inch blossoms in almost all colors. They do best in rich deep soil in cooler climates. The roots suffer in heat and dryness. Sweet peas should be planted in a deep trench with very rich soil. The seeds should be treated with a special culture of nitrogen-fixing bacteria. See your local nursery for this.

SWEET WILLIAM: See **DIANTHUS**

WAX BEGONIA: Wax begonias grow 10 to 12 inches tall with pink, red, and white flowers in 2-inch clusters. They generally flower well all summer. They grow slowly from seed, and are better grown from seedlings. Set out the seedlings after the last frost. Begonias prefer light shade and rich moist soil. You can dig them up before the last frost and use them as houseplants.

ZINNIA: Zinnias are tender annuals with showy flowers, growing to about 1 to 3 feet high. They are easy to grow, although they don't do well in cooler climates and are perennials in warmer climates. Sow them indoors in peat pots about a month before the last frost. They are warm-weather plants that prefer good soil and full sun. Feed and water regularly, taking care to keep water off the leaves.

3

PERENNIALS

Perennials are plants that do not die at the end of each growing season, but renew themselves year after year. Some perennials are grown as annuals in climates where they will not survive from year to year. Generally speaking, trees, bushes, and grass are perennials, but gardeners use the term to refer to herbaceous flowering plants that live 3 years or more. Plants that generally live only a year are annuals, while those that live 2 years are biennials. These terms refer more to gardening practice than to unchangeable characteristics of a particular plant. What is a perennial in Alabama may be a biennial in Nebraska and an annual in Minnesota. Perennials include chrysanthemums, peonies, and irises. Some bulbs and bulblike plants are also perennials, but they will be discussed separately.

Although perennials grow from year to year, they are not care free. They require regular care, including feeding, staking, and cutting back. Many require regular dividing and replanting. Perennials do not bloom through the season like annuals. Many flower only for a few weeks, although some bloom for as long as two months. For a full flower garden, perennials must be planned so that one variety is flowering as another loses its blooms. Most people prefer to combine perennials with annuals to ensure a constant supply of blooms.

In planning your garden, keep in mind when various perennials bloom. Some, such as irises and Oriental poppies, bloom in the spring and early summer. Daylilies, phlox, and others bloom in the summer. Still other perennials, such as asters and chrysanthemums, bloom in the fall. A careful combination will give you a full season of flowers.

Most perennials require full sun for at least 6 hours a day, although spring-flowering perennials prefer part shade. All require good drainage, and do not do well near tree roots.

SOIL PREPARATION AND PLANTING

Soil preparation should be done in the fall for best results. Soil should be prepared deep: at least a foot, preferably 18 to 24 inches. Weeds should be removed and soil loosened, adding manure and peat moss. It is also a good idea to add phosphate and potassium. Do a good job, keeping in mind that the perennials you are going to plant will be there for years to come, and you will not have another chance to work the soil.

Perennials are difficult and slow to grow from seed. The easiest way is to buy clump divisions from a nursery. Plant them when they start to show signs of life. Avoid buying plants that are already growing. Most should be planted with the crown right about soil level. Peonies should be planted in a deep hole with the buds 1 to 2 inches below soil level. Make sure that the hole for each plant gives the roots plenty of room. Be sure to press down the soil so that no air pockets remain.

After a few years, many perennials will require dividing. This is usually done in early spring. Dig up the roots, pull or cut the clump in two, and replant the two new clumps. Add plenty of potassium and phosphate when replanting. Perennials are best propagated through division. This ensures that the new plants will run true to the original. Perennials planted from seeds can vary greatly in color, size, or shape from the plant that produced the seed. If planting from seed, use only certified seeds from a reputable dealer.

Many tall perennials, such as delphiniums, require staking. Perennials usually require little special watering, and care should be taken to avoid getting water on the leaves. Most perennials benefit from a good feeding at the beginning of their spring growth, using a fertilizer with 10 to 15% nitrogen. This will encourage growth and blooming. Water regularly during the growth and blooming period. After blooming, remove old blossoms and stems. Clean up the plants in the late fall when old leaves and stems have dried up. In very cold areas, mulch in the winter, especially if the ground is not frozen and snow-covered throughout the winter.

COMMON AND POPULAR PERENNIALS

ACHILLEA: See **YARROW**

ARTEMISIA: Some species are more noted for their white or silver mounds of leaves than for their flowers, and some are aromatic herbs. They prefer dry, well-drained soil and full sun. Avoid overwatering. Artemisia are easily divided. This should be done in spring and fall.

ASTER: Asters are generally fall bloomers, but some hybrids bloom in spring. There are over 600 species, with a very wide range of colors. Asters can grow anywhere from 1 to 6 feet tall. They do best in full sun and fertile soil with regular watering. Asters should be divided every few years in late fall or early spring. Replant the outer clumps and discard the older center.

ASTILBE: Astilbe bloom from early to late summer in pink, red, and white plumelike flowers. They prefer cool, moist, but well-drained soil with plenty of organic matter. They do best in partial shade in hotter climates, full sun where it is cooler. They generally require frequent dividing.

BALLOONFLOWER: Bell-shaped flowers, either single or double. Balloonflowers bloom in midsummer. They prefer full sun, but will grow in partial shade in hotter climates. Balloonflowers do best in moist but sandy soil. They generally don't require dividing. Pick off faded or dead blossoms to encourage growth.

BELLFLOWER: There are over 300 species with a wide variety of shapes and sizes and blue, purple, or white flowers. The species include perennials, biennials, and annuals. They generally bloom in early summer through fall. Bellflowers prefer full sun, but grow well in partial shade in hot climates. They prefer moist, well-drained soil. The clumps should be divided every 3 to 4 years.

BERGENIA: Bergenias have large leaves, often up to a foot wide, and big clusters of delicate spring blooms. The two basic varieties are the heart-leaved bergenia and the leather bergenia, which has oval leaves. The leaves stay green year round in the south. Bergenias grow well in most soil, and prefer full sun except in hot climates where they do better in partial shade. Divide the clumps every 3 to 4 years, planting about a foot apart.

BLANKETFLOWER: A perennial with daisylike flowers in red, yellow, and gold, although some are annuals. They grow up to 3 feet tall and do well in hot dry climates. They are easy to grow from seed and require good drainage. Blanketflowers are summer bloomers, lasting for a long time. They don't do well in high humidity.

BLEEDING HEART: Bleeding heart varies greatly in size (1 to 3 feet tall) and blooms from spring to fall depending on variety. It prefers partial shade, light moist soil, and good drainage. It is short-lived in areas with mild winters. Bleeding heart goes completely dormant in winter, so be

careful to avoid digging up the plant by accident when
working the garden again in the spring.

BUTTERFLY WEED: Butterfly weed produces showy
bright orange flowers for a few weeks in summer. The
blossoms are very attractive to butterflies. The plants grow
from 1 to 3 feet high. It prefers sandy soil with good
drainage and full sun. It has a deep taproot and doesn't
require much water.

CHRYSANTHEMUM: There are many species of chrysanthemum, including Shasta daisy, hardy chrysanthemum, and
marguerite. Some less sturdy chrysanthemums are grown
as annuals, particularly in cooler climates. Chrysanthemum
produces round flowers that vary from very small to very
large, and the plants range from 1 to 4 feet high. The
flowers come in a wide range of colors, especially red,
white, lavender, and pink. The cut flowers last a very long
time. Chrysanthemums don't winter well in cold climates.
Many chrysanthemums bloom so late in the year that they
are not recommended for gardens, doing better indoors or
as greenhouse plants, particularly in cooler climates. Check
with your local nursery to see which varieties do best in
your area.

Divide the plants in spring, planting side shoots and discarding the center of the clump. For huge blooms, remove
all but 1 or 2 buds from each cluster. They prefer full sun
and good well-drained soil with plenty of organic matter.
Dig in a balanced fertilizer several weeks before planting. Regularly pinch back the top pair of leaves on any
shoot over 6 inches long. Larger plants may require staking. After the plant has bloomed, cut it back to within 6 to 8 inches of the ground. Hardy chrysanthemum
require more care than most, doing best if replanted every
year.

COLUMBINE: Dainty flowers and leaves, with flowers of
nearly all colors. Columbine blooms in mid to late spring,
growing from 6 inches to 3 feet, depending on variety. It
does well in full sun or part shade. Columbine prefers well-
drained soil and regular watering. Cut back the old stems

to encourage a new crop of flowers. The plants should be replaced every 3 to 4 years.

CONEFLOWER: Coneflower has bright flowers and is easy to grow. The most common variety is the black-eyed susan. It blooms in mid to late summer. The plant grows in clumps that need to be divided every few years. Most varieties prefer full sun and do well in any type of soil.

CORAL BELLS: This plant has tiny bell-shaped flowers, usually pink or red, growing on thin stems rising up from mats of leaves. It prefers moist soil with good drainage and full sun, although it does well in partial shade in warmer climates. It works well as an edging or border flower, since the leaves stay green year round except in very cold climates. Divide the plants every 3 to 4 years. Use the younger root divisions, discarding the old, woody rootstock.

COREOPSIS: Some species are perennials, others are annuals. A member of the sunflower family, it produces daisylike yellow flowers. It blooms in the summer, growing 1 to 3 feet high depending on variety. It prefers full sun and does well in fairly infertile soil. Remove old flowers to encourage growth. The perennials can be planted from seed or by division of the root crown.

DAYLILY: Daylilies are not true lilies, which are grown from bulbs. Different varieties of daylily bloom from late spring to early autumn. They produce a wide variety of colors, varying from 2 to 4 feet high. Both tall and dwarf varieties are available. They prefer full sun, but can tolerate partial shade, particularly in hotter climates. They do well in average soil with good organic matter. They can go some time without dividing, but should be divided before clumps become very large. Divide in late fall or early spring. These are very good for cut flowers.

DELPHINIUM: Some species are short-lived and are grown as annuals, particularly in cold climates. They can grow over 5 feet tall, with large spikes of flowers. They prefer full sun, but do better in cooler climates. Protect from strong wind if possible, and stake plants when they attain their full height. Delphinium prefers rich, alkaline soil. Add lime to your soil if it is very acid. Water and feed delphiniums regularly. They will bloom in late spring and again in the fall if the spring flowers are cut off before the seed pods develop. After fall blooming, cut back the spikes to the bottom foliage.

DIANTHUS: Dianthus includes perennial pinks and carnations, as well as biennial sweet william. They bloom for a long time, and their cut flowers are long lasting. Most garden varieties grow to about 18 inches tall. They grow best in full sun with light, sandy, well-drained soil. Do not mulch dianthus.

FOXGLOVE: Also called digitalis, some species of foxglove are biennials. They produce rose, yellow, purple, or white tubular flowers on tall spikes, growing up to 8 feet tall. Sow directly in the garden in spring or set out plants in the fall. They prefer fertile, well-drained soil with lots of organic matter, and full sun or partial shade. Cut the stems of dead flowers to encourage growth, and divide regularly. After the first flowering, cut off the main spike. The plant will continue to flower from side shoots until early fall.

GAS PLANT: This is a sturdy long-lived plant that does well in cooler climates. It blooms in late spring or early summer, with spikes of pink or white flowers on tall stems. They are said to give off gas on humid nights that can be ignited, and that can cause allergic reactions if touched. Gas plant prefers moist, well-drained soil in sun or partial shade. It forms thick clumps that should not be divided.

GAYFEATHER: Gayfeather blooms in late summer or early fall, with pink or white plumes of wavy flowers on a tall spike, growing 2 to 6 feet tall depending on variety. It prefers deep, light soil and full sun. Once established, it tolerates heat, cold, and drought. Gayfeather produces good cut flowers.

GERANIUM: These perennials are hardy geraniums, as opposed to a tender perennial usually referred to as geraniums. It produces five-petaled flowers an inch or more across, in pink, purple, lavender, and blue, and near-evergreen leaves. Geraniums bloom from late spring to midsummer. They prefer full sun but tolerate light shade, particularly in hot climates, and do best in moist but well-drained soil. Geraniums form large clumps that do not have to be divided, but can be.

GLOBEFLOWER: Globeflower produces light yellow to dark orange flowers similar to buttercups, and dark green leaves. They bloom in late spring or early summer, averaging 2 feet, but growing up to 4 feet. They prefer partial shade, but can tolerate full sun. They grow best in rich soil with plenty of moisture. They can be divided, but don't require it. Globeflower produces very good cut flowers.

HIBISCUS: Hibiscus is a relative of the hollyhock. It produces very large pink, white, or red flowers, ranging up to 12 inches across. They reach their largest growth in extremely moist soil. The plants can grow up to 8 feet high. Hibiscus prefers full sun and grows in any soil. They should be planted about 3 feet apart, with the root crown about 3 inches below the soil. Propagation of plants is difficult. The average gardener is better off buying plants or growing from seed.

HOSTA: Also known as plantain lily, hosta has unusual leaves with a wide variety of sizes, colors, and markings. The leaves are typically heart-shaped with shiny veins. White or lavender bell-like flowers bloom in late summer. They make very good edging plants. Hosta does well in shade or partial shade. It prefers moist, well-drained soil and regular watering. Feed once a year with a balanced fertilizer. The plants divide easily.

IRIS: There are over 200 species of iris. Most flower in spring or early summer. They have 3 petals that stand upright and 3 petals that hang down. The most common varieties are the bearded iris, which have hairy tufts hanging from the 3 petals that hang down (the falls). They come in a wide variety of colors, growing 2 to 4 feet high. The bearded iris blooms in late spring. Other types are daintier and bloom later. They prefer full sun in cooler areas, partial shade in warmer climates, and require good drainage. Plant irises in late summer in the north, early fall in the south. Remove old leaves in the fall, and mulch in very cold areas.

LUPINE: Different types of lupine are perennials, annuals, and shrubs. They produce tall spikes of flower clusters, 2 to 4 feet tall. The plants may require staking. Most varieties prefer cooler climates. They prefer deep rich soil and sun to partial shade, and require good drainage. Lupine are generally not long lived. Plant from seed in the early spring, soaking the seeds in hot water overnight first.

MONKSHOOD: Monkshood is difficult to grow in hot, dry climates. It produces tall spikes of blue flowers. All parts of the plant are poisonous. It prefers partial shade, but can tolerate full sun, particularly if the soil is kept moist. It is important to water regularly, not letting the soil dry out. Monkshood prefers cooler climates. Sow directly in the garden in spring. Division is not recommended. They are best grown from seed.

PANSY: See **VIOLA**

PEONY: Virtually all peonies are hybrids. There are two basic types, herbaceous and tree peonies. The herbaceous peonies produce large, round, short-lived flowers in a mound of dark green leaves about 3 feet high and just as wide. They require a good winter chill. They don't like a hot dry spring, but do well in a hot summer once established. Plant herbaceous peonies in early fall with the tuber eyes no more than 2 inches below ground. They may require some support. Cut the stem back to below ground level in the fall.

Tree peonies, actually a shrub, grow to about 5 feet high and wide. Plant in the fall in deep, well-drained, rich soil. These have less need for a good winter chilling than the herbaceous varieties. They are hardy, but the flowers may have to be protected from strong winds. They do best in partial shade in hot climates. Plant in fall or early spring, keeping them away from tree roots. Remove faded or dead flowers regularly to encourage growth. Cut the plants back to live wood in the spring when the buds begin to swell.

PHLOX: Phlox varieties include both annuals and perennials. Some have evergreen foliage. Garden phlox are the most common, growing 2 to 4 feet high with big clusters of flowers blooming in midsummer. Other varieties are smaller and bloom earlier. They prefer light fertile soil with plenty of organic matter and full sun. Plant about 18 inches apart. When the shoots are about 6 inches high, thin the plants to about 4 to 5 shoots per clump. Divide the plants every few years.

PINKS: Also known as dianthus, there are over 300 species of pink, including carnations and sweet williams. The flowers are usually pink, but sometimes white or red. The flowers look like small carnations. They bloom in spring or early summer, usually growing from 6 to 18 inches tall. They require very good drainage, and care should be taken not to overwater. Remove faded or dead flowers to encourage growth. Divide the clumps every few years. Don't divide mat-forming varieties. (See also **DIANTHUS**)

POPPY: Some varieties of poppy are best grown as annuals. Oriental poppy is a perennial that blooms for a few weeks in late spring or early summer. They produce large, showy flowers that leave a tall messy-looking stem after blooming. It is best to plant them where other plants will hide the poppies after blooming. Poppies grow in average soil with good drainage and light watering. They prefer full sun except in very hot climates. Start the plants from root cuttings in late summer, planting about 18 inches apart. Remove faded or dead blooms. Poppies do not require division.

PRIMROSE: There are over 600 species of primrose. Some short-lived varieties are grown as annuals. Primrose blooms in the spring, producing 6-inch clusters of

1-to-2-inch flowers, some with evergreen leaves. They prefer partial shade and moist, slightly acid soil. Primrose does not generally do very well in very hot climates. It grows best in the Pacific Northwest, particularly in Washington and Oregon. Some species can be grown in warmer climates. Check with your local nursery for more information as to what can be grown in your area. Plant primrose about 6 to 12 inches apart. Divide the plants every other year, immediately after flowering. All but the newer hybrids are easier to grow from seed.

SCABIOSA: Also known as the pincushion flower, it produces white or blue lacy flowers resembling a pincushion. They grow 18 to 30 inches tall, blooming in early to late summer. Scabiosa can flower into early winter in warmer areas. It prefers full sun except in very hot climates, and moist soil with good drainage. It generally doesn't need division. Cutting the flowers encourages growth.

SEA-LAVENDER: Some varieties are annuals. Sea-lavender produces dainty lavender flowers on long thin stems. It blooms for a long time in summer. Sea-lavender prefers full sun and well-drained sandy soil. Divide regularly. It makes a good cut flower, and it keeps its color when dried.

SHASTA DAISY: This is a species of chrysanthemum. It is easily grown from seed, producing white flowers that bloom for a long time in summer and fall. It prefers rich, moist soil with good drainage. It does best in full sun except in very hot climates. Water regularly, especially when blooming. Pinch back in early summer. Do not divide until clumps are well established, usually after 2 to 3 years. Set out in fall or early spring. Mulch in colder areas, taking care not to smother the foliage.

VERONICA: Veronica generally produces blue flowers on spikes, but can be white, pink, or lavender. It prefers sun, but will tolerate partial shade. It requires moist soil with good drainage, and should be watered regularly. Divide in spring or fall. The mat-forming varieties require less care.

VIOLA: Viola includes sweet violet, viola, and pansies. Sweet violet grows about 8 inches tall with small flowers. Pansies grow about the same height, but have 2-to-3-inch flowers. Violas are similar to pansies, but slightly smaller. Pansies are grown as biennials in hot climates. All three are good for cut flowers. They do best in light shade and moist soil with plenty of organic matter.

YARROW: Also known as achillea, yarrow produces flat clusters of flowers, usually yellow. It has fernlike leaves, with a hint of gray. Yarrow is long blooming in summer, growing to about 2 to 3 feet tall. It prefers full sun and well-drained soil, and doesn't require a lot of water. Yarrow needs to be divided regularly when the clumps get crowded. The taller species make good cut and dried flowers.

4

BULBS

The term *bulb* is commonly used to cover a wide variety of flowering plants that includes true bulbs, corms, rhizomes, tubers, and tuberous roots. The distinction is not particularly important for the casual gardener who is just interested in planting and growing flowers. What these plants have in common is that each is a complete system consisting of the plant and its food-storage mechanism that can survive extreme conditions.

There are two basic types of bulbs, spring blooming and summer blooming. Most spring-blooming bulbs do not have to be dug up again after planting. The major exception is in warm climates where winters are not cold enough to make bulbs go dormant. There, nontropical bulbs must be dug up and refrigerated for several months before being returned to the ground. Summer bulbs are more tender and can't tolerate winter. In cold climates, the summer bulbs have to be dug up and kept inside over the winter. Spring-blooming plants should be planted in the fall, while summer-blooming bulbs should be planted in the spring.

Bulbs prefer full sun, and must have very good drainage.

If bulbs get too wet for too long, they rot and die. Also, the warmer the soil, the earlier the bulb will bloom. Spring-blooming bulbs tend to be hardier than summer bloomers, and will grow in most any soil. Bulbs do best in slightly acidic soil. Have your soil tested, and add limestone to light soil if needed. If your soil is very alkaline, add ground sulfur or iron sulfate.

To plant, dig a hole about four times deeper and four times wider than the bulb itself. Work some good bulb fertilizer into the bottom of the hole, put in the bulb with the pointed side up, and replace the soil. Bulb fertilizer is high in phosphorus and low in nitrogen. Bone meal is an excellent bulb fertilizer. A good balanced fertilizer for bulbs would be a 5–10–5 mix. In colder climates, planting a little deeper will protect the bulb against the cold and prevent it from sprouting too early.

Bulbs require little care. They can be dressed with some compost in the early spring and early fall. Once well established, they should be divided periodically. Do not cut back the foliage after the blossoms have faded. In this stage, the plant is making and storing food to start next year's spring growth. The leaves should not be removed until after they turn yellow.

COMMON AND POPULAR BULBS

ANEMONE: Also called windflower, these plants flower in the spring and grow up to 18 inches tall. The blossoms open in sunlight and close up at night or when it is very cloudy. They prefer full sun, but can tolerate partial shade, particularly in hotter climates. They grow best in light soil with organic matter and good drainage. Add some lime if the soil is acidic. Soak the tubers up to 48 hours before planting.

BEGONIA: Growing up to a foot high, begonias produce large flowers with vivid colors. The stems are fragile and they should be planted out of the way of traffic. Do not get the leaves wet, particularly if they are out in the sun. They should be very well drained. Excess water can result in rot. They do best in bright light but out of the direct sun, moist soil with plenty of organic matter, and humid but well-circulating air.

The tubers are best started indoors in midwinter in peat moss. Water lightly. When sprouts appear, put each in a 5-inch pot filled with potting soil. Feed every few weeks with a high-nitrogen liquid fertilizer. When the nights warm up and there is no danger of frost, move them outside or plant them in good soil about a foot apart. Stop watering in late summer and dig them up after the foliage has died. Store in dry peat until time to replant.

BUTTERCUP: These bulbs produce flowers 3 to 5 inches across, blooming for up to 4 months. They come in a wide range of colors and are usually grown for cut flowers. A single plant can produce more than 50 flowers in a season. They prefer full sun and moist soil. They should be planted in early spring in the north, and in late fall in the south.

Soak the tubers in warm water for several hours before planting. In cooler climates, the bulbs should be dug up and stored indoors for the winter. Divide the tubers after the foliage has died.

CANNA: Cannas grow from 2 to 5 feet high, producing foot-high spikes of 4-inch blossoms. They bloom from early summer until the first frost. They do best in moist soil with plenty of organic matter, and they prefer full sun. In warmer climates, plant directly in the garden in spring. In cooler areas, start cannas indoors in peat pots about a month before warm weather. Plant them about a foot apart and feed them every few weeks with a balanced fertilizer such as 5–10–5.

In cooler climates, cut down the stalks after they have been blackened by frost, and dig up the roots and let them dry. Store upside down in peat moss. Propagate by dividing the rhizomes in early spring.

COLCHICUM: Also known as autumn crocus. This plant produces foliage but no blooms in spring, and by summer the foliage is gone. Then in the fall, stems appear, without leaves, followed shortly by flowers. The flowers look something like crocuses, but are not related.

Colchicum corms should be planted in late summer or early fall. They prefer full sun or partial shade and moist soil. Add organic matter to sandy soil to hold moisture. Plant about 9 inches apart, with the top of the bulb 3 to 4 inches below the ground.

CROCUS: Many crocus bloom early, often poking up out of the snow. Others are fall bloomers. They are hardy and do well in cool climates. Spring bloomers prefer full sun but will tolerate partial shade, and need well-drained soil. Fall bloomers prefer cooler, shadier locations. Plant in the early fall, about 4 inches deep and 4 inches apart. Apply a light feeding of bone meal or a 5–10–5 fertilizer. Crocuses multiply by themselves and need not be divided. If they are planted in or near grass, take care not to mow the leaves while they are still green. They can be planted from seed, but take 3 to 4 years to reach full growth. Therefore most gardeners buy and plant corms.

CYCLAMEN: Cyclamens have flowers on long stems above heart-shaped leaves. The most common variety grows best in warm climates or as a houseplant in the north. It blooms from late fall to early spring and is dormant in the summer. Other types can grow in milder northern climates.

Plant the corms when dormant in midsummer, about a foot apart and 2 inches deep. They prefer partial shade and moist but not wet soil.

DAFFODIL: See NARCISSUS

DAHLIA: Dahlias vary greatly in size, shape, and color. They range from 1 to 7 feet tall, and the flowers can be anywhere from 1 to 12 inches across.

Dahlias prefer full sun or light partial shade, in rich soil, particularly in potassium and phosphorus. The tuberous roots must be dug up every fall in climates with frost.

Plant the roots about the time of the last frost, laying them flat in a hole about 6 inches deep. Cover with a few inches of soil, adding more soil as the plant grows. For short bushy plants, pinch them back when they reach about a foot high. After a frost or two, gently dig up the roots, cutting back the stem to 2 inches. Store in peat in a very cool place. Divide in spring before replanting by slicing vertically through the stem.

GLADIOLUS: Glads produce tall spikes of brightly colored flowers that last a long time after cutting. They grow best in full sun and rich, sandy soil. Plant after the last frost, planting more every few weeks for a long blooming season. Plant the corms about 5 inches deep and about 6 inches apart. Top-feed with a balanced fertilizer when they first come up and again after picking.

After first frost, dig up the plant and cut back the stem to about an inch. Dry for a few weeks and break off the old corm. Dust with fungicide and store in a cool dry place.

GLORY OF THE SNOW: Although they bloom shortly after crocuses, they too might be seen poking through the snow. They have small star-shaped blue flowers and grasslike foliage.

Glory of the snow prefers full sun except in hotter climates, where partial shade is better. They do best in rich, moist, but well-drained soil with some organic matter. Plant in early fall, about 3 inches apart and 3 inches deep.

GRAPE HYACINTH: These have small spikes of tiny blue flowers, rarely reaching a foot in height. They prefer full sun and well-drained soil. Plant in late summer or early fall, planting about 3 inches deep and 3 inches apart.

HYACINTH: Hyacinth has a sweet aroma, and some varieties produce flower clusters up to 10 inches high. In colder climates, hyacinth should be planted in early fall. In warmer areas, the bulbs should be refrigerated for a month and planted in late fall. They do best in slightly sandy soil, moist but well drained, and prefer full sun. Plant the bulbs about 6 inches apart and 6 inches deep.

IRIS: There are over 200 species of iris. Iris grows from rhizomes, from fibrous roots, and from bulbs. The first two are perennials and are discussed in Chapter 3.

Varieties of bulb iris range from 4 to 18 inches tall, with a wide variety of colors. They do not do well in the north, where they have to be dug up in late summer and stored over the winter.

Plant in early fall. Iris prefers full sun, light soil, and very good drainage. They do better in partial shade in hotter climates. Plant smaller varieties about 4 inches apart and 4 inches deep. The large Dutch iris should be planted 6 inches apart and 6 inches deep. After about 4 to 5 years, the blossoming will decline. At that time, dig up the bulbs and replant them farther apart.

LILY: These are true lilies, unlike daylilies, which grow from rhizomes. They bloom from early summer to early fall, ranging in height from 2 to 8 feet. There are a great number of hybrids, with a wide range of colors and shapes. They tend to be tall and gawky, and often have to be staked.

Lilies grow wild in very poor soil, and overfeeding tends to give them weak stems. They need some moisture, but require very good drainage. Lilies can be planted in the spring or fall, about 6 inches deep and a foot apart.

LILY OF THE VALLEY: These plants produce stalks of tiny white bell-shaped flowers. They grow well as ground cover in shady areas of the garden, and make good cut flowers. They do not grow well in very hot areas. They prefer partial shade and moist slightly acid soil. Plant in the early spring, spacing them about a foot apart and covering with about an inch of soil. Mulch in the fall. Propagate by division in the fall when the leaves have turned yellow.

NARCISSUS: There are many varieties of narcissus (the plural is narcissi), including what are commonly referred to as daffodils and jonquils. They vary greatly in size and color.

Narcissus prefers full sun or very light shade, with sandy soil and good drainage. Plant about 6 inches apart and 6 inches deep, adding fertilizer with a high phosphorus content. Divide every 4 years or so by digging up the plant after the foliage has died and pulling apart the bulbs that come apart easily.

NASTURTIUM: Nasturtiums bloom in summer, producing inch-wide flowers and deep leaves. Some varieties grow up to 6 feet high by twining. They prefer partial shade. Plant them in the spring, about a foot apart, and cover with 2 to 3 inches of soil. In cooler areas, the tubers should be dug up in the fall and stored indoors in peat moss. Propagate by dividing the tubers in the fall.

TULIP: There are three major types of tulip, distinguished according to when they flower during the growing season: early, middle, and late. Check with your nursery for the many types of tulips, and to see which bloom best in the various parts of the season in your area.

Tulips prefer full sun except in very hot climates, where partial shade is better. Plant in early to middle fall, about 6 inches deep, adding bone meal to the soil. They do best in sandy, well-drained soil. When the shoots appear, top-dress with 5–10–5 fertilizer. Keep the bulbs cool before planting. In warmer climates, refrigerate the bulbs for 3 to 4 weeks before planting.

5

ROSES

Roses are shrubs with woody stems and a reputation for being hard to grow. With proper care, you can grow roses relatively easily, and have long blooming flowers year after year. Just make sure that you buy the best varieties for your area, plant them correctly, and give them proper care.

There are many different types of roses, with a wide range of colors and sizes. The most familiar is the hybrid tea rose. There are thousands of varieties of tea roses, with new ones being introduced every year. Hybrid tea roses grow on bushes ranging from 3 feet to over 7 feet tall, with red, pink, yellow, white, orange, peach, or salmon flowers. Hybrid teas are not the hardiest of roses, although some varieties do better than others in cooler climates. Check with your local nursery for the types that do best in your area.

Floribundas are smaller and hardier than hybrid teas. They usually grow about 2 to 4 feet high and can be used for hedges. They produce a lot of flowers in clusters, and grow in the same range of colors as the hybrid tea roses. Grandifloras are a cross between floribundas and hybrid teas. They are very large plants, growing as high as 9 to 10 feet. Grandifloras produce a lot of flowers that are good for cutting.

Miniature roses are very small, with plants ranging from 6 inches to a few feet. They come in most of the same colors as hybrid teas and do well as potted plants indoors. The so-called old roses include moss roses, cabbage roses, Chinas, and teas. They are usually more fragrant than the modern hybrids, but more delicate and harder to grow.

Climbing roses do not have vines that twist around and stick to other things. Rather, they send up woody canes whose thorns hook other vegetation. These vertical canes then send out horizontal runners that produce flowers. Climbing roses do not do well in cooler climates.

Roses prefer full sun and do best with an eastern exposure where they get the full effect of the morning sun. They do well in most soils as long as they have good drainage, and do best if they have good air circulation. Do not plant close to trees or shrubs where they will have to compete for water. Work in plenty of organic matter such as compost or moist peat moss. Plant roses in early spring in cooler climates, and in winter in very warm areas. Roses can be purchased by mail order or at a good local nursery. Avoid supermarkets or other sources. Mail-order rose plants will arrive dormant and with bare roots. Soak them in water for at least a day and plant immediately. Always buy Number 1 plants, which means that they have three or more canes at least 18 inches high. Most roses require some protection during the winter in cooler climates.

Plant roses in a hole about 2 feet wide and deep enough for the root system. Space them about 2 feet apart in general, more for particularly large varieties, less for particularly small ones. Remember that the plants will be smaller in cooler climates and larger in warmer areas when spacing. Take care not to let bare root plants dry out. Plant these on a mound in the center of the hole, draping the roots down the side of the mound. Cut back any broken roots or canes to below the break. Most roses are hybrids and have an enlarged bud at the base of the stem where it was grafted. In warm climates, plant with the bud just aboveground. In cooler climates, plant with the bud an inch or so below the soil. Larger plants may need some support, such as a trellis.

Roses should be watered deeply several times a week, taking care not to get the leaves wet. The exception is in hot dry areas, where occasional overhead watering washes off dust and pests. For deep watering, build a basin around the plant and flood it, or use a drip system or a soaker hose. Water in the morning to avoid diseases. Weed roses regularly by hand, and avoid using herbicides. Feed roses with a balanced liquid fertilizer after the first bloom and again in late summer. Check with your local nursery to see if there are pests or diseases in your area that attack roses, and follow their advice for prevention.

Feed roses with a complete commercial fertilizer as soon as growth begins. Give additional feeding after each blooming period ends. Stop feeding about 6 weeks before the first expected hard frost of the season, usually late summer to early fall. A dry commercial fertilizer applied directly to the soil works best.

Prune roses in the early spring, cutting away dead canes. Prune a little at a time, checking the center of the cane as you cut it. If the center is brown, the cane is dead. When you reach white center, stop pruning. You probably want to cut back even healthy canes that are long and straggly to make the plant more attractive. Cutting the canes back to about a foot and a half gives a compact shrub with good air circulation. This will promote flowering.

Remember that roses bloom on new growth. Prune the plants at the end of the dormant season, when the buds are just starting to swell. Remove all dead wood and cut back any long spindly twigs. Remove any suckers that have sprouted from the rootstock. On well-established plants, cutting flowers is a form of pruning. Cut off just enough stem to support the flower in a vase, leaving as much foliage on the plant as possible. Roses also benefit by pruning deadheads, cutting off faded blooms that remain on the plant. Cut back to an outward-facing bud that is just above a leaf stem with five leaflets on it.

In colder areas, where temperatures regularly get below 10 degrees, roses need to be protected against winter. Water the plant well, then build up a mound of dirt 6 to 12 inches high around the base of the plant. In the spring, check under the dirt mound for new growth. When it appears, remove the dirt. An alternative method of protection is to put up a small barrier around the plants, using wire fencing, snow fence, etc., and cover the plants with mulch.

6

VEGETABLES

Contrary to what some people might believe, the term
vegetable is not a scientific classification. Everyone knows
about the tomato being a fruit. This is because the *fruit* is the
part of a plant that contains the seeds. And the fruit of the
tomato plant is the part that we eat. We also eat the fruit of
the pepper plant. And the eggplant. Try telling someone that
pepper is a fruit. *Vegetable* is just a catchall name for those
plants that we eat that aren't sweet (we call those fruit) and
that aren't grain. The part of the plant that we do eat also
varies from one vegetable to another. We eat the leaves of
lettuce and cabbage and other greens. We eat the bulbs of
onions and the roots of carrots and beets. Potatoes look like
roots, but it is actually an enlarged part of the stem that we
eat. Cauliflower is a flower, as is broccoli.

Something else that most people believe, and that usually
is true, is that homegrown vegetables are often much more
expensive than going down to the supermarket. Unless you
are growing vegetables on a fairly large scale, by the time
you add in seed and fertilizer and tools and your time, you

would be much better off stocking up your grocery cart down at the produce section. That's not why most people grow vegetables.

People grow vegetables for the fun of it, and to control the pesticides used on them, and mostly to walk out in the garden and pick something fresh for tonight's dinner that tastes a lot better than something that has spent the last week in a truck coming across the country.

The major considerations in deciding what vegetables to grow are what you like and what grows well in your part of the country. If you are just starting out, check with your local nursery to see what does well in your area. And start out with vegetables that are very easy to grow and require little or no special care. These include lettuce, radishes, beets, and tomatoes.

Knowing your local growing season is very important for planting vegetables. If you live in a cold climate, you may have to start some plants indoors to grow them successfully. Fall crops that take too long to ripen can't be planted in very cold areas. Longer growing seasons may allow you to plant a summer crop after a spring harvest. Any late-ripening vegetables must be harvested before the first frost of the fall. The amount of daylight can also be an important factor. Certain plants do better with longer days and will grow better further north, where it stays light longer during the summer.

Don't plant too much, particularly when starting out with your vegetable garden. Start out small, find out what grows well in your area and how much time and work it takes, and expand gradually from there. You will also have to learn how much garden space each type of vegetable requires for health and growth. This also varies with climate.

A vegetable garden is best situated in a sunny spot with good drainage. Don't plant vegetables too close to trees or shrubs. The roots of the larger plants will take water and nutrients away from the vegetables, and the shade will stunt the growth of the smaller plants. Ideally, the soil should be good loam, neither sandy nor heavy clay, loose and fertile. If your garden spot is dictated to you by circumstances, do as much as you can to make it look like the ideal described above. It is best and easiest to prepare the soil for a vegetable garden in the fall, particularly if you have a lot of work to do with the soil. The soil should be tilled about 8 inches deep. Use a spading fork to work a small plot of ground. For a large garden, you may want to rent a rototiller. Work in a balanced and complete commercial fertilizer as you till the soil. Use about 5 pounds of 5–10–5 per 100 square feet, or about half that much 10–10–10.

Plant seeds directly in the garden at a depth of about 3 to 4 times the diameter of the seed. Avoid forming a hard crust of dirt over seeds that are very small or slow growing. Keep the seeded area moist until the seedlings appear. Seeds can also be started indoors in almost any kind of container and replanted outdoors when the weather is right. The easiest way is to start seeds in peat pots. When it is time to set out the plants, just put the whole thing, pot and all, in the ground. This is not only easier for you, but it also avoids transplant shock to the plant.

In colder areas, you can start plants outdoors using a cold frame. This is essentially a wooden box or frame that sits over a patch of garden ground. It has a hinged lid, most of whose surface is glass or plastic to let light in. The hinge allows the top to be propped up to let in warmer air and closed when it is cold, particularly at night.

The timing of planting is important both to ensure the best growth for the plant and to get the maximum enjoyment out of the harvest. Where possible, you will want to plant certain vegetables in batches several weeks apart so that the harvest is spread out over a month or more, enabling you to pick a little at a time.

TYPES OF VEGETABLES

ASPARAGUS: Asparagus is a perennial, coming back each year without being replanted. It prefers full sun, but will tolerate some shade. The soil should be well prepared and well fertilized. Use a lot of manure, bone meal, and potassium. Asparagus requires a dormant season, and does not grow well in areas such as the Gulf Coast, which has moist soil and moderate winters.

Asparagus takes a long time to grow from seed, and does not produce a crop until the third year. Start seeds indoors about 3 months before the last frost, and set out when the plants are about a foot high. It is much easier to buy year-old roots from a nursery. These will produce a crop after 2 years. Plant the roots in the fall in a warm climate, in the early spring in a cool climate. Plant in rows, digging a trench about a foot deep and a foot wide. Space the roots a foot and a half apart. Make a mound of soil around each root, with the top of the mound about 6 inches below the ground level, and the root tentacles hanging over the top of the mound. Then fill in the trench with enough soil to cover the root tips with about 3 inches of soil. As the asparagus grows gradually fill in the trench.

Keep the young plants well watered and weed often. Don't pick any asparagus the first year. Cut down the plants when the foliage dies in winter. You probably won't get any asparagus big enough to pick the second year either. After that, pick finger-sized spears in the spring, until the weather turns hot and the spears start coming up thin. Ripe spears are about 8 inches long with tightly compressed tips. To pick the spears, just bend the stem until it snaps off.

BEANS: There are many different varieties of beans, but they are all planted in pretty much the same way. Beans prefer full sun and good drainage, and loam soil with lots of organic matter. They don't need a lot of fertilizer, particularly not nitrogen. Legumes, including beans, draw their nitrogen from the air.

There are dozens of varieties of beans. Check with your nursery for recommendations about what does well in your area. String beans, also known as snap beans, can be green or yellow (called wax beans). Both green and yellow beans can be either bush beans that grow short, or pole beans that grow on long vines. Bush beans grow quickly, producing beans about 6 weeks after the last frost. Pole beans take longer to produce, but keep producing until the first frost. Shell beans, such as lima beans or soybeans, also take a long time to produce. They grow best where summers are long and hot.

Bean seeds are sown directly in the ground when there is no danger of frost. Plant about an inch deep, moistening the soil and not patting it down too firmly. Pole beans will require support, so plant them where you can put some poles or a trellis.

Pick string beans after they are about as thick as a pencil. Keep picking them to increase the production. For shell beans such as limas or soybeans, let the beans in the pods get big and lumpy.

BEETS: Beets are cool-weather biennials that are easy to grow and quick to mature. They will tolerate some shade, and prefer a sandy soil with some organic matter added. (Compost works better than manure.) Sow in early spring, soaking the seeds if the weather is dry. Plant the seeds about ½ inch deep and about 1 inch apart. You can plant more every few weeks to get a steady production through the season.

Keep the soil around the seedlings moist, and thin them out when they are about 2 inches high. Pull out seedlings so that they are about 4 inches apart, and snip all but one in each cluster. Water well and weed regularly. When the plants are about 4 inches high, add a 5–10–5 fertilizer along the sides of the plants.

The greens can be picked off of growing beets and cooked. Harvest the root when it is about 3 inches in diameter, usually about 9 weeks after sowing.

BROCCOLI: Broccoli is a relative of the cabbage that grows well in full sun, but does not need it. It also does well in cooler climates. It does need good drainage and air circulation. Broccoli likes rich soil, especially when young, particularly nitrogen and calcium. To avoid disease, it should not be planted in soil that has grown broccoli or any other member of the cabbage family for 3 years.

Broccoli can be sown directly in the garden in early spring. Plant the seeds in groups of 3 to 4 per hole, ½ inch deep, and about a foot apart. When the seedlings are an inch high, thin each group by cutting out all but the single strongest plant. It is easier, however, to plant seedlings obtained from a nursery. Space seedlings 12 to

18 inches apart, adding rotted manure to each hole. Soak the soil well whenever it dries out.

Harvest the first bunch after it has formed in the center of the plant, just before the buds open. This will be about 4 to 5 weeks after sowing. New bunches will then grow around it. Keep harvesting as the bunches mature, or the plant will start to send out yellow flowers and stop producing.

BRUSSELS SPROUTS: This is a cool-climate plant that grows slowly and produces late in the season. It is a relative of cabbage, and should not be planted in soil that has been used to grow brussels sprouts, cabbage, or any other member of that family in the last 3 years. It is very resistant to cold, and can be harvested late into autumn. Brussels sprouts prefer full sun and good drainage, and should be shielded from the wind, as they blow over easily. They like a deep sandy loam with relatively little nitrogen.

In a cooler climate, start seeds indoors and set out, planting about 3 months before hard frost. In warmer climates, 2 crops are possible. Sow in February for harvesting in midspring, and sow again in early summer. Plant about 2 feet apart, and mulch to keep the soil moist. Fertilize with a commercial fertilizer such as 5–10–5 scattered along the sides of the plants when they are 6 inches high, again when a foot high, and a third time just as the sprouts form. Harvest sprouts when they are about half the size of a golf ball, usually after about 4 months.

CABBAGE: Cabbage takes a lot of garden space to grow. It prefers cool temperatures and full sun, but will grow well in partial shade, and likes rich soils with lots of organic matter. Cabbage and related plants are subject to diseases, particularly if planted in the same soil year after year. Cabbage, brussels sprouts, broccoli, and any other member of the cabbage family should not be planted in soil that was used to grow the same or any other related plant within the last 3 years. You will need 2 to 3 square feet of garden for each head of cabbage.

It is possible to grow 2 crops in a season, if the first crop is started indoors. Start the seeds about six weeks before the last frost in a cool sunny place indoors. Set the plants out about 3 weeks before the average last frost. Set them out deeper than they were in their seedling pots, with soil up to the leaves. Sow late crops directly into the garden in mid-July.

Soil should be moist but not wet. If the head starts to crack down the middle, sending up a seed stalk, it is getting too much water or the soil is overly rich. If the cabbage head does crack, you need to slow down its growth. Take the head, turn it one half turn, and pull up enough to slightly dislodge the roots. An alternative method is to shove a spade into the ground in a couple of places about 6 inches from the plant, severing the roots. Harvest the cabbages when fully formed and still firm.

CARROTS: Carrots prefer cool weather. They don't do well in temperatures above 90 degrees. In hotter climates, carrots should be grown in the fall or spring. In the north, they can be planted in early spring, planting more every few weeks to maintain production. Carrots prefer full sun and good drainage, but will grow well in partial shade. They grow best in loose, sandy moist soil. Manure should be dug into the ground at least 6 months before planting. The soil should be high in potassium and phosphate and low in nitrogen.

Sow the seeds directly into the garden about 3 weeks before the last frost. Water the seeds and cover with mulch, taking care to keep them moist. Thin the plants when they reach 2 inches high so that the seedlings are about an inch apart. Thin a second time to about 2 inches apart when the plants start to look crowded again. This second time, thin by harvesting the small carrots, which can now be eaten. Fertilize the plants by applying a 5–10–5 commercial preparation along the sides when they are about 4 inches high and again at 8 inches.

CAULIFLOWER: Cauliflower prefers full sun and good drainage, and doesn't grow well in either very hot or very cold weather. The soil should be rich and should not have been used to grow this or other cabbage family plants for 3 years.

In cooler climates, cauliflower should be planted indoors about 2 to 3 months before the first frost. Plant in late spring to early summer, depending on your area. For spring crops in warmer areas, start seeds indoors about 5 weeks before setting plants out. Set out plants when they are about 6 inches high. Plant cauliflower about 2 feet apart, building a rim or basin of soil around the plant to hold water. Use cutworm collars (such as a paper cup with the bottom cut out) as a barrier against insects.

To sow directly in the garden, plant groups of 4 to 5 seeds ½ inch deep and 18 inches apart in rows 3 feet apart. When the plants are about an inch high, thin each group by removing all but the strongest plant. Fertilize every 4 weeks with a commercial preparation of 10–10–10 along each side of the rows.

Cauliflower cannot tolerate dryness. Keep the soil moist, soaking the ground at least 6 inches down. Using a mulch will help. Cauliflower heads need to be "blanched" or they will turn green and not taste as good. When the head is about the size of a golf ball, bend over the large green leaves around it to cover the head, tucking them in on the other side and breaking the leaf ribs so that they won't spring back. If necessary, tie the leaves together with string or a rubber band to keep light and moisture out but let some air in. Make sure that the head is dry, and water around but not on the plant. Harvest when the heads are about 6 inches across and firm.

CELERY: Celery takes quite a while to grow, with a 5-to-6-month growing season, and it does not like very hot weather. It prefers very wet soil and partial shade. (Wild celery grows in marshes.) Celery is easier to grow from seedlings than from seed. If growing from seed, start indoors about a month before the last frost. Transplant to peat pots when the seedlings are 2 inches high. Set out about the time of the last frost, spacing about 6 to 8 inches apart. Plant in a trench, leaving the crowns a little below ground level. Fill in the trench as the celery grows. Water well and cover with mulch.

Fertilize the plant every few weeks with a weak solution of liquid fertilizer. Celery can be harvested a stalk at a time from the outside of the bunch, or cut off the whole bunch when it is mature.

CHARD: Generally called Swiss chard, this plant is a relative of the beet but is grown for its leaves rather than for its roots. The plants grow up to 1½ feet high, with red or green crinkled leaves. A single planting can be harvested over a 3-month growing season.

Seeds should be sown directly in the garden about 2 weeks before the last frost. Plant about an inch deep and 4 inches apart, in rows about 18 inches apart. When the seedlings are 6 inches tall, thin the plants to about 8 inches apart. The thinning may be eaten. Feed about once a month with a 5–10–5 commercial fertilizer. Harvest the outer leaves when they are about 8 inches high, usually 2 months after planting.

COLLARD: Collards are a typically southern plant, also called tree cabbage. It looks like a cabbage when young, but soon develops a stem up to 4 feet high. Collard is a cabbage relative, and should not be planted in soil used to plant itself or any related plant within the last 3 years. Sow seeds directly in the garden in early spring as soon as the soil can be worked. Plant 3 to 4 seeds in a group, thinning to 1 plant per group when the seedlings are about an inch high. When the plants reach about 5 inches high, pull out every other plant. Thin again until the plants are about 3 feet apart. The thinned plants can be eaten. Feed the plants about once a month with a commercial 10–10–10 fertilizer.

CORN: Corn does not have a very extensive root system, so it can be planted in a relatively small area. It does best in full sun and should be sheltered from strong winds, which can blow it over. It prefers rich soil, particularly in nitrogen. It is sown directly in the garden about the time of the last frost. You may want to stagger the planting to have corn ready to harvest over a period of time.

Plant about 6 inches apart, and then thin out to about a foot apart. Top-dress with high-nitrogen fertilizer when about 8 to 10 inches tall, and again when the stalks develop tassels. Water well, watching for dried, rolled-up leaves as an indication that the plant needs more water. Corn needs to pollinate itself, so don't plant different varieties next to each other. Harvest when the ears are large and dark green with brown tassels. Test by peeling back the husk and sticking your fingernail into a kernel. If milky liquid spurts out, the corn is ready.

CUCUMBERS: Cucumbers prefer warm weather, but no overly dry heat. They grow to maturity in about 2 months. They grow on sprawling vines, and need about a square yard per plant. They grow best in clay soil with plenty of humus.

Presoak the seeds and plant after the last frost. When the seedlings are 2 to 3 inches high, thin out to a foot apart. Mulch to keep the soil moist and to give the plants something to rest on as a protection against disease.

Cucumbers must be picked when they are ripe. If left to yellow on the vine, they will stop producing. Check the seed packet for harvesting size.

EGGPLANT: Eggplants require very warm weather, with temperatures above 55 degrees at night and over 80 degrees during the day for a 2-to-3-month growing period. They grow up to 3 feet tall, with each plant producing up to 4 fruits. The fruit grows up to 10 inches long, but tastes better when eaten at about half of the maximum growth.

Eggplant should not be grown where tomatoes, potatoes, or eggplant has been grown within the last 3 years. Start seeds indoors about 10 weeks before the hot weather needed to sustain growth. When the seedlings are about an inch high, transplant them into peat pots. Keep them warm and moist at all times. When night temperatures are consistently above 55 degrees, set the plants out into the garden, spacing them about 2½ feet apart in rows 2½ feet apart. Feed with weakly diluted liquid fertilizer and protect from cutworm with paper cups with the bottoms cut out. Feed monthly with a 5–10–5 commercial fertilizer.

Pick the fruit when it is about 6 inches long and very shiny. This is usually about 1½ months after setting plants outdoors. Pick all fruit before it matures, or the plant will stop producing.

ENDIVE: Also called escarole, endive looks like lettuce but has a slightly sharper flavor. Sow seeds in midsummer, about 3 months before first frost, aiming for a fall harvest. Plant the seeds in groups of 3 to 4 about ½ inch deep and a foot apart in rows 2 feet apart. When the seedlings are about an inch high, thin out to leave only the strongest plant in each group. Fertilize about once a month with a commercial 10–10–10 blend along the bases of the plants.

Endive needs to be blanched (protected from the sun) to remove its bitter flavor. When the plants are about 15 inches across, gather the outer leaves together and bind them with a rubber band. The leaves are ready for harvesting about 3 months after sowing.

ESCAROLE: See **ENDIVE**

GARLIC: Garlic is a relative of the onion, growing up to 2 feet high with small clusters of tiny white flowers. It needs full sun and does best in slightly sandy soil with plenty of organic matter. Plant cloves of garlic in early spring, about an inch deep and 6 inches apart. When the plants are 6 inches high, feed with a commercial 5–10–5 fertilizer. Dig up the bulbs when the foliage dies down in the fall. (See also **ONIONS**)

LEEKS: Leeks are a milder member of the onion family. They do not form bulbs, but grow long stems up to 2 inches in diameter and 8 to 10 inches long. Sow indoors about 2 months before the last expected frost. Set the plants out in the garden when they are about 4 inches high, planting them in a trench about 6 inches deep and 6 inches wide. Space the plants about 6 inches apart. Feed about once a month with a commercial 5–10–5 fertilizer. Leeks are edible at earlier stages, but mature at about 4 months. They will keep after harvesting for up to 2 years.(See also **ONIONS**)

LETTUCE: Lettuce does not grow well (if at all) in extreme heat or full sun. It grows quickly and prefers nitrogen-rich, sandy soil. Sow directly in the garden as soon as the soil can be worked. Moisten the area, sow seeds very thinly, and cover with a light dusting of soil. Use mulch to keep the soil moist. Top-dress occasionally with nitrogen-rich fertilizer.

Head lettuce is usually harvested by the head, but any lettuce can be harvested leaf by leaf as needed.

OKRA: Generally thought of as a southern vegetable, okra does best in hot climates but will grow in the north. It prefers full sun and light, well-drained soil with lots of organic matter. Work compost or rotted manure into the soil when planting. In warm climates, sow directly into the garden after soaking seeds overnight. In the north, start indoors in peat pots about 6 weeks early for planting in early June.

Plant seeds an inch deep and thin later to 18 inches apart. Keep soil moist and use mulch. Top-dress every 2 to 3 weeks with a balanced fertilizer. Pick the pods after the flowers drop off. Keep picking, every day if needed, to keep the plant producing.

ONIONS: This family includes all varieties of onions as well as leeks, shallots, garlic, and chives. Onions can be grown from seed, from seedlings, or from sets. Seeds take a long time, especially in the north. Sets are small immature bulbs, dried and ready to plant. This is the easiest method, but sets are rarely available for anything other than basic yellow onions.

Check with your local nursery to see what varieties do best in your area. The length of summer days in your area is at least as important as average temperature. Some types of onions do better in the longer summer days of the north. Onions that prefer shorter days do better in the south.

Onions prefer full sun and must be kept weed free. A well-balanced fertilizer works best, and the ground does not have to be prepared very deep. Sow directly into the garden in very early spring, or even in the autumn before the growing season. Sow the seeds in a wide, well-moistened furrow and cover with an inch of soil. As the onions grow thin them to about 4 inches apart. Eat the thinning as green onions (scallions).

Start seedlings indoors in late winter, keeping them cool and moist. Set them out when they are about 6 inches high, trimming the tops by about 3 inches. Plant 4 inches apart in a furrow. Keep plants moist and well weeded. Mulching helps with both tasks. Apply a balanced fertilizer next to the plants occasionally, avoiding excess nitrogen.

The onions are ready to harvest when the tops fall over. Pull them up, leave the tops on, and dry them, in the sun if possible. Otherwise lay them out in a warm, dry spot. After the onions are dry, store them in a mesh bag, or braid the tops together and hang them up.

Leeks are part of the onion family, resembling large scallions. They can be eaten when scallion size, or grown to full size and cooked. Grow them just like onions, but harvest by digging them up instead of pulling them out of the ground. Harvest as needed.

French shallots are another onion-family member, but they are easier to grow. Just buy shallots and pull apart the clusters to make sets for planting. Plant in early spring in northern areas and in the fall in the south. Harvest when the leaves die down. Dry and save in the same way as onions, saving some for next year's planting.

Garlic is also a member of the onion family. Simply buy some garlic, separate the cloves, and plant each one with the point up. Plant in the early spring in the north, in the late fall in the south. Avoid overfeeding and overwatering. Harvest when the tops have died. Dry and store in mesh bags or braid the tops together and hang.

PARSNIPS: Parsnips look somewhat like white carrots and add flavor to soups and stews. They are slow growing and take some time to produce. Salsify (sometimes called oyster plant) is related and is grown the same way. Scorzonera, referred to as black salsify, which it resembles, is not related but is also grown like parsnips. Parsnips prefer deep soil with plenty of organic matter, moderately light and not too sandy. Make sure that all rocks and roots have been removed. Avoid fresh manure and excessive nitrogen.

Sow the seeds directly in the garden as soon as the soil can be worked, soaking the seeds overnight in warm water. Plant in a well-moistened furrow, sowing the seeds thickly, and cover with ½ inch of soil. Take particular care in keeping the plants weed free, and don't let the soil dry out.

Parsnips are best if left in the ground for a freeze or two.

Even better, harvest half your crop after a few freezes and leave the rest in the ground over the winter, covering with mulch. Harvest as soon as the ground is soft enough in the spring to pull them up.

PEAS: Peas cannot tolerate hot weather, but they can handle frost. Since they produce quickly, they are ideal for planting in early spring or fall. In the south, peas can be planted in the fall to lie dormant over the winter and harvest in the spring.

Spring planting should be in light sandy soil, while a later planting should be in a soil with a little more clay to keep the roots cooler. The soil should have plenty of organic matter and should be moist but well drained.

Peas grow on vines that require support. If you have a wire fence around your garden, plant peas next to the fence. Otherwise you will need to use stakes or trellises. For early crops, plant the seeds about an inch deep, preferably in raised beds for better drainage. Later crops should be planted in a deep, well-moistened furrow and covered with 2 inches of soil. Plant the seeds 1 or 2 inches apart. Apply fertilizer when the plants are about 6 inches tall, avoiding excessive nitrogen.

Pick green peas when you can feel full, round peas in the pod, but before the peas turn hard. Peas with edible pods are picked before the peas form fully, while the pod is still flat but full-sized. Peas need to be eaten or frozen immediately after picking.

PEPPERS: There are dozens of varieties of peppers, ranging from sweet to red-hot. Most require a warm climate and do best in hot weather. Peppers prefer full sun, and sweet and hot peppers should not be planted close together, or they can cross-pollinate. They grow well in average sandy loam with balanced fertilizer.

Peppers are best started indoors about 2 months before the last frost. Plant the seeds in peat pots and keep the seedlings warm. Do not set out until the nights are fairly warm (lows in the 50s). Slit the sides of the peat pots and plant about 18 inches apart. Feed every few weeks with a balanced liquid fertilizer. Harvest anytime you want by cutting the pepper with clippers. If picked small and green, the pepper will be hotter. As they get larger and turn red the pepper will be mellower. Keep picking the peppers to maximize the plant's production.

POTATOES: Potatoes can be planted from the eyes of grocery-store potatoes, but for best results buy disease-free seed potatoes from a nursery. Potatoes prefer sun, but don't require full sun. They do best in rich, well-drained, well-aerated soil with little clay.

Cut the seed potatoes in quarters and plant in a shallow trench, mounding more soil around the plants as they grow. Plant 2 to 3 weeks before the last frost, but make sure that the ground is fully dried out. Potatoes can be harvested after the foliage dies, making sure to dig them all up before a heavy frost. Immature ("new") potatoes can be dug up anytime, but these are for immediate eating. Potatoes need to mature fully before they can be stored. Don't wash potatoes that are to be stored, and keep them in a cool dark place with good ventilation.

RADISHES: Radishes require little space and mature quickly. They do best in full sun, but can tolerate some shade. They prefer a sandy loam with good moisture. Sow directly in the garden, checking the variety for planting dates in your area. You can plant more every few weeks for continuing production. When the plants are about 2 inches high, thin them to about 4 to 6 inches apart. Keep well watered and weed free. Fertilizer is generally not needed. Harvest as soon as full-grown. Radishes do not keep well in the ground or store well after being harvested.

RHUBARB: Rhubarb is a perennial vegetable, coming up again every year and requiring little if any attention. It is a large plant and requires a lot of room. The typical plant is about 3 feet wide. The stalks are eaten; the leaves are poisonous.

Rhubarb does not do well in hot, dry weather, preferring cooler climates with hard frost in the winter. It prefers a deep, well-drained soil with a lot of manure or compost. Rhubarb is usually planted from divisions of existing clumps. Plant in the early spring as soon as the soil can be worked. Plant with the crown of the plant about 2 inches below the soil, spacing the plants about 3 feet apart.

Do not harvest any stalks the first year, just cut back the flowers. The next spring, feed with liquid fertilizer and keep well watered. In the summer, the plant will produce tall, thick stalks with whitish flowers. Cut these off at the base. Harvest some thicker stalks the second year, but leave most to develop the plant. You can harvest a few more the third year. After that, you can harvest almost as much as you want.

SPINACH: Spinach prefers cooler weather, and it does best as a spring or fall crop. Long sunny days in particular cause it to stop producing. Plant spinach in partial shade, especially in hot climates. It needs a lot of organic matter and fertilizer, particularly nitrogen. Sow seeds directly into the garden, as soon as the ground can be worked for a spring crop. Plant the seeds about ½ inch deep and an inch apart. As soon as leaves appear, thin to 4 inches apart. As the plants grow, thin again to about 9 inches apart. Use the thinning for salad greens. Top-feed with a high-nitrogen fertilizer when the plants are 6 inches tall. Harvest by cutting outside leaves as you need them.

SQUASH: Squash grows on vines and on bushes. There are two major types, summer squash and winter squash. The summer type has white or yellow flesh and is harvested in summer while still immature. Winter squash have orange flesh and are good for storage. Most winter squash grow on vines, but some grow on bushes.

Summer squash needs full sun. Winter squash will grow in partial shade. Either variety needs to be planted in a small mound or hill. To plant, dig a hole about 18 inches deep and just as wide. Put about 4 inches of compost in the bottom of the hole, then fill with a mixture of 3 parts soil and 1 part compost. Make a mound of this mixture about 4 inches high. Space the mounds about 5 feet apart for bush squash, and about 10 feet apart for vine squash.

Plant 6 to 8 seeds an inch deep in each mound. When the

plants are 3 inches high, thin out all but the strongest two. As they grow feed with a commercial 5–10–5 fertilizer.

SWEET POTATOES: These plants take up a lot more room in your garden than white potatoes. They do best in warm-to-hot climates, preferring full sun and good drainage. Plant in slightly sandy soil with low-nitrogen fertilizer. These potatoes are grown from tuber sprouts called slips. Plant about a foot apart, with 4 inches of the slip in the ground. Water well when first planted, then avoid overwatering as the plant matures. Dig the potatoes when the foliage yellows and dies. Take care not to allow the potatoes to freeze.

TOMATOES: There are dozens of varieties of tomatoes. Check with your local nursery for the types that do best in your area, and for the varieties that best suit your tastes and purposes. There are three main types of tomato plants. Determinates are short and bushy, growing 12 to 18 inches high and producing 1 crop per season. Semideterminates are a little larger, growing up to 2 feet high. Like determinates, they stop producing when they reach full growth. Indeterminates have long vines, and produce until stopped by frost. Determinates are easiest to grow and tend.

Tomatoes prefer full sun and warm, well-drained soil. The soil should be loose with plenty of organic matter. The best way to grow tomatoes from seed is to start them indoors in peat pots. Set them out after the last frost, planting the top of the pot 2 inches below soil level. The seedlings should be short and bushy with no flowers. Let the pots sit outside for a week before planting to get the plants used to cooler weather. Prepare the soil with a commercial 5–10–5 fertilizer, setting the plants 2 to 3 feet apart. To plant from seed, sow groups of 3 to 4 seeds 2 to 3 feet apart. Thin the seedlings when they are an inch high.

Indeterminates can be left to sprawl on the ground, but they do better, and your garden looks neater, if you support them with stakes, cages, or a trellis. Keep tomatoes well watered and top-feed with a liquid fertilizer at least once during the season. Prevent cutworm damage by placing a paper cup with the bottom cut out over each plant. Harvest the tomatoes when they are fully red. If they are not ripe when the weather turns cold, you will have to harvest everything before the first hard frost. Put the tomatoes in a cool dark place, one layer deep, discarding any that have holes, cracks, or rot.

TURNIPS: Turnips are a strong-flavored root vegetable, with greens that can also be cooked and eaten. They prefer cool weather, and they get tough and go to seed in very hot weather. Turnips do best in loose, well-drained soil with plenty of organic material.

Spring turnips can be planted as soon as you can work the soil, and fall turnips can wait up until late summer, even in the north. Sow directly in the garden, spacing the seeds about an inch apart. When the seedlings reach 6 inches, thin them out to about 4 inches apart, using the thinning as greens. Turnips need to be weeded often. Harvest when the root bulb is about 2 or 3 inches in diameter. Cut off the tops and store in a cool dry place.

7

❧~❦~❧

HERBS

Herbs are soft-stemmed plants whose leaves are used for flavor in cooking. You can grow enough herbs for home use in a relatively small space, but herbs tend to spread quickly and take over a lot of room if left alone. Snipping herbs regularly for cooking tends to make them grow more compactly and tastier. The wide variety of herbs includes annuals, biennials, and perennials. Annuals can be grown almost anywhere. Biennials require a cool rest period between the first and second season. Perennials also grow in most areas, but do not do particularly well in southern Florida or on the Gulf Coast. Herbs can be grown anywhere: by themselves, with vegetables, with flowers, or in pots in the house for winter use.

Herbs generally prefer full sun, and herbs grown indoors do best with a growing light. Annuals are best started indoors about 4 to 6 weeks before the last expected frost. Plant three or four seeds per container, and thin to the single strongest plant when the seedlings show their first true leaves. Transplant outdoors after all danger of frost has passed. Perennials generally grow well from seed, and will provide useful leaves in the first year, although it is better to wait until the second year before harvesting. Sow seeds directly in the garden anytime after early spring, keeping the soil slightly moist until the seedlings develop true leaves. At this time, thin the plants to about 8 inches apart.

Herbs can be grown in most any type of soil, but do best in average, well-drained soil enriched with lots of organic matter. Most herbs growing outdoors can be dug up and potted to bring into the house for the winter. In general, herbs are harvested a little at a time as needed for cooking. If the plant is very big, or if it is the end of the growing season, you may want to, or have to, harvest the whole thing. Herbs are best used when they are fresh, but they can be dried for future use. Hang the herbs upside down so that the flavorful oils run into the leaves, with a plastic bag to catch falling leaves and seeds.

COMMON HERBS

ANISE: Anise is an annual herb, grown for its licorice-flavored seeds. It grows up to 2 feet high and has tiny lacy leaves and 2-inch clusters of flowers. Anise needs full sun and well-drained soil. Anise has a growing season of about 4 months, so it must be planted as soon as possible after the danger of frost is past. Plant the seeds about 2 inches deep, and thin the plants to 6 to 8 inches apart when the seedlings reach about 2 inches high. Harvest when the seeds turn pale gray.

BASIL: Basil is a tall plant with big green leaves. The leaves can be used whole in salads or pureed to season Italian sauces. Basil grows best in full sun in loose well-drained soil. Sow the seeds directly in the garden after the last frost. Pinch back the plants when they are about 6 inches tall, and pinch off any flowers that start to bloom. Basil is best dried on trays in a well-ventilated place. It can be frozen or used in herb vinegar.

CARAWAY: Caraway is a biennial grown for its licorice-flavored seeds. The plant grows about 8 inches high its first season and reaches about 2 feet the second year. In this second season, it produces tiny white flowers that ripen into brown seeds in midsummer. The plant dies after the seeds have ripened. Caraway can be grown in most parts of the country, although it does not do well in Florida or along the Gulf Coast.

Caraway grows best in full sun and well-drained soil. Sow the seeds directly in the garden, about ⅛ inch deep. When the seedlings are 2 inches high, thin the plants to about 8 to 10 inches apart. Harvest the seeds when they turn brown.

CHERVIL: Chervil is a hardy annual, growing up to a foot high, that looks something like parsley. It prefers partial shade, particularly in hot climates. Sow the seeds directly into the garden as soon as the soil can be worked. Thin the seedlings to about 6 inches apart. Harvest before the flowers open, drying or freezing the herb.

CHIVES: Chives are hardy perennials, related to onions but usually with a milder taste. They grow up to a foot high, with small clusters of purple flowers. Chives prefer full sun, but grow well in partial shade. They like moist but well-drained soil with plenty of organic matter. They can be grown directly from seed, but will take a long time to produce. Chives are easier to grow by dividing an existing clump. Plant the divisions about 2 inches deep and 6 inches apart. In most parts of the country they should be planted in the spring, but in very hot climates, plant in late summer for a winter harvest.

Chives can stay green outdoors throughout the winter, even in northern climates. Harvest the leaves for use at any time. This encourages growth. Chives are best fresh, but can be frozen or even dried if necessary.

CORIANDER: This is a hardy annual with a strong flavor. The upper leaves look like dill and the lower leaves look like parsley, but it doesn't taste like either. It is called cilantro in Spanish and dhania in India. It is also called Chinese parsley. It grows 2 to 3 feet high with fernlike foliage.

Coriander grows well in full sun or partial shade, preferring fertile, well-drained soil. Coriander does best if it is sheltered from strong winds. Sow seeds directly in the garden after the last frost. Thin the seedlings to about a foot apart when they are 2 inches high. Coriander grows quickly, and you can make successive plantings through the summer. Cut the leaves anytime for cooking. It is best to harvest the leaves before the plant blooms and dry the leaves.

DILL: Dill is an annual that grows up to 5 feet tall with wavy blue leaves. It goes well in salads and with fish. Its yellow flowers can be used in bouquets. Dill prefers full sun and moist but well-drained soil with plenty of organic matter. It does best if sheltered from strong winds. Sow directly in the garden in early spring, or in late summer for next year's crop. When the seedlings are about 2 inches high, thin the plants to a foot apart. When the plants are a foot high, feed with a commercial 5–10–5 fertilizer. Dill tastes best fresh, but it can be dried or frozen in plastic bags.

FENNEL: Fennel is a perennial that is often grown as an annual. It is grown for its licorice-flavored leaves and seeds. Fennel grows up to 4 feet high with feathery foliage and small clusters of yellow flowers. It needs full sun and will grow in almost any soil. Sow directly in the garden in early spring, barely covering the seeds with soil. When the seedlings are 2 inches high, thin to about a foot between plants. When the plants reach a foot high, feed with a commercial 5–10–5 fertilizer. The leaves may be picked at any time and should be harvested when they begin to turn brown.

MARJORAM: Sweet marjoram is a perennial, but it is usually grown as an annual. It grows up to a foot high with tiny white flowers. Sweet marjoram requires full sun and prefers a slightly sandy soil. Sow directly in the garden in the spring, thinning to 6 inches apart. Pick leaves and stems at any time for immediate use. Harvest the leaves when the plant blossoms.

MINT: Mint is very strong and should be used sparingly if at all. It is a hardy perennial that grows up to 3 feet tall. Mint can spread rapidly and widely, and can quickly take over a garden. To keep mint from spreading, you need a barrier around and often under the plant. One method is to bury a large coffee can or a small bucket in the garden with a few drainage holes in the bottom, fill with dirt, and plant the mint inside the container. The mint will eventually get out, but it will take a while. The best way is to plant mint only in a pot.

Mint prefers partial shade and moist soil. Pinch back the stems occasionally and snip off any flowers to encourage growth. (Mint is very hard to kill. You can cut it off at ground level or even pull it out at the roots and it will spring right back.) Cut mint as needed. Let the leaves dry on the stems until crumbly, then pick, dry further and store in plastic bags or airtight jars.

OREGANO: Oregano, and its milder relative marjoram, prefer full sun and light, well-drained soil. Both should be divided every few years after the stems become woody. For best taste, harvest before the plant blooms. Dry hanging upside down in a brown paper bag, crumbling the leaves when fully dried.

PARSLEY: Parsley is a hardy biennial that self-sows and grows well in most climates. It is generally grown only for the leaves that it produces in its first year, and then dug up. Parsley prefers full sun, but does well in partial shade. Sow directly in the early spring, soaking the seeds overnight before planting. Thin the seedlings to about 3 inches apart when they are 2 inches high. As the plants begin to touch, thin again so that they are about a foot apart. Feed with a commercial 5–10–5 fertilizer when the plants are about 4 inches high, and again about a month later. Snip the outer leaves as needed. Dry by hanging upside down in a dry, well-ventilated place.

ROSEMARY: This is an evergreen perennial in warmer climates, and is best grown as a potted plant in very cold areas. It grows up to 6 feet high in the south. It prefers full sun and can tolerate poor soil as long as it is very well drained. It is difficult to grow from seed. It is much easier to buy small plants from your nursery. Pick the leaves for use anytime. Rosemary is best fresh, but keeps its flavor well when dried hanging in a paper bag.

SAGE: Sage is a perennial that grows 2 to 3 feet tall and prefers full sun and very well-drained soil. It can be grown from seed, but is easier to grow from a small plant. Plant about 2 feet apart. Cut the plants back once or twice a season to keep them from taking over the garden. Harvest the leaves just before the plant flowers, hanging them in bunches to dry. The plants weaken after about 5 years and should be removed.

TARRAGON: This is a hardy perennial, growing up to 3 feet tall. French tarragon is what most people are familiar with. Other varieties, such as Russian tarragon, do not taste the same. Tarragon prefers full sun but can tolerate some shade, and does better in well-drained, mildly sandy soil. French tarragon is not usually grown from seed. Purchase a plant from a nursery and divide it every few years. Feed the plants in early spring and again in early summer with a commercial 5–10–5 fertilizer. Pick the leaves for use anytime. Propagate from root divisions in early spring.

Harvest the leaves during a dry period and hang them upside down in a paper bag. Store the dried leaves in airtight jars or freeze in plastic bags. Tarragon can also be used to make vinegar, but it is best used fresh.

THYME: Thyme is a hardy perennial, a woody shrub that also produces aromatic flowers. The plants grow up to a foot high, and they are often used for edging. Thyme grows best in full sun and sandy, well-drained soil. If the soil is heavy, add organic matter. Thyme is best grown from divisions of existing plants. Set the plants out about a foot apart. Pick the leaves for use anytime. Just before blooming, harvest the thyme in sprigs and hang them upside down in a dark, dry place. Strip off the leaves when dry and store in airtight jars. Divide the plants every 3 to 4 years.

8

FRUIT

Fruit usually grows on bushes or trees, taking up a lot more space than flowers or vegetables. It is much more important to pick the right type of fruit for your region and climate than it is with other plants. Check with gardening friends or with a good local nursery to see which kinds of fruit do best in your area. Also remember that some fruit plants are self-pollinating, while others need a different variety of the same kind to pollinate and produce fruit.

Most types of fruit trees are now available in dwarf or semidwarf varieties. These are usually a graft of a standard variety of the tree onto the rootstock of a genetic dwarf. Dwarf trees require much less space and produce fruit sooner than their standard-size relatives. Semidwarf fruit trees are larger than dwarfs, but smaller than standard-size trees. The smaller trees have proportionally smaller root systems, and may not do as well under adverse conditions.

Different fruit trees do better in different parts of the country. Apples, peaches, and plums do not do as well in the south, because they do not get the rest they need during their winter dormancy. Citrus trees are difficult if not impossible to grow in cooler climates because of the winter cold. A late spring frost can kill the early buds on any fruit tree. Early-flowering trees should be planted on a north-facing slope so that the early spring sun does not stimulate early budding.

For best results, buy and plant fruit trees that are 2 years old, and about 3 to 5 feet high. These younger trees are less sensitive to the shock of transplanting than more mature trees. Except for citrus, fruit trees are best planted when they are leafless and dormant.

In the north, plant fruit trees in the early spring as soon as the soil can be worked. In hotter climates, it is better to plant fruit trees in late fall or winter, allowing the trees to become well established before they have to contend with a long hot summer.

To plant a fruit tree, dig a hole at least half again as large as the tree's root system. Mix in 1 part peat moss for each 2 parts of soil. Do not fertilize young trees until they are well established. The roots of younger trees are sensitive to overfeeding and to chemical burn. When planting dwarf or semidwarf trees, make sure that the graft is above the ground.

Newly planted fruit trees should be pruned immediately. Cut off any weak-looking growth, as well as any oddly shaped or poorly placed branches. You need to remove about half of the tree's top growth to make up for a similar loss of roots when the tree was dug up. Water the tree regularly throughout the first summer.

Fruit trees need less feeding than other trees or shrubs. Excessive feeding tends to encourage branch and leaf growth, at the expense of fruit production. When fruit begins to appear, it also needs to be thinned for optimal output.

COMMON AND POPULAR FRUITS

APPLES: Apple trees can be grown in most parts of the country, but they do best where the temperature stays between 20 and 40 degrees for most of the winter. The trees live 30 to 40 years and are most productive after age 10. Most apple varieties are not self-pollinating and must be planted near other varieties. Certain varieties, such as Jonathan and Golden Delicious, are known as good pollinators; others, such as Winesap, are not. Early-bearing apples tend to taste better, but don't keep well. Midseason apples are generally good for both eating and cooking. Late-bearing apples are better for cooking, and keep well over the winter.

Apple trees are generally easy to grow, ranging from 20 to 40 feet high at full growth, but numerous pests and diseases make it difficult to get a big crop of good-looking apples from a tree. Apple trees are also routinely grafted onto dwarf rootstock to produce miniatures, about 6 feet high; dwarfs, about 10 feet high, and semidwarfs in the 15-to-20-foot range.

Dwarf trees take up much less space (you can plant 5 to 10 dwarfs in the same space as a single full-size tree) and the fruit tends not to bruise as much, not having as far to fall. The smaller trees also produce fruit sooner. Dwarfs usually produce fruit within 2 or 3 years of planting, and semidwarfs within 3 to 4 years. On the other hand, dwarfs have a shallow root system, so that they usually have to be staked, and don't do well in cold climates. Check with your local nursery to see which varieties do best in your area.

Apples prefer full sun with good drainage. They shouldn't be planted on steeply sloping ground. And don't plant apple trees at the bottom of a big slope or in a valley. Cold air tends to flow down into such valleys at night, producing frost pockets that can kill buds in early spring. Soil should be deep with plenty of organic matter, avoiding heavy clay.

Apple trees should be planted in the early spring in the north. In warmer climates, they can be planted whenever they are dormant. Apple trees should be planted as far apart as the expected height of the tree. Thus true dwarfs should be about 6 feet apart, while full-size trees need to be about 30 to 40 feet apart. Trees should be planted when young, 1 to 2 years at most. Cut back the branches after planting, saving only a half-dozen branches with the best placement.

It is best to cover the shallow root system with mulch, particularly while the tree is young. This holds in moisture while protecting against cold. Straw or shredded bark works well. Do not feed the tree for the first year, and top-feed after that with a fertilizer rich in nitrogen. It is best to feed early in spring. Prune the tree annually when it is dormant (winter or early spring), cutting off very low branches and allowing light into the branch system from above. Heavy branches at the top will put the lower branches in permanent shadow and they will never bear fruit.

Apples are particularly prone to pest damage, including apple maggots and coddling moths. Check with your local nursery to see which pests are a problem in your area and what to do about them. These pests attack the fruit. There are also a number of diseases that attack the tree itself. These include apple scab and cedar apple rust. Apple scab shows up as dark spots on leaves and twigs. Treat it with dormant oil spray, available at your nursery. Avoid cedar apple rust by not planting apple trees and red cedar near each other.

When the tree starts to produce fruit, the apples themselves must be thinned out for the best fruit production. Some apples will drop off naturally in early summer. The rest should be thinned out when they have attained about one third of their full size. Thin the apples out so that they are about 6 to 8 inches apart. Apples are ready to pick when they look ready and pull off easily. Late-maturing apples may have to be harvested early to avoid frost damage. Apples should be stored in a dry cool place, not piled very deep. Don't store apples that are cut or bruised.

APRICOTS: Apricots do best in areas that have long summers, but they also require freezing weather during their dormant period. They should not be planted near tomatoes, melons, raspberries, or strawberries, all of which can transmit disease. Apricots prefer deep, fertile, well-drained soil, avoiding excess clay or sand. Some varieties, including Moongold and Sungold, require trees of other varieties nearby for cross-pollination.

Apricots should be planted as 1-to-2-year-old trees, planting 20 to 25 feet apart for full-size trees. Dwarfs will grow to about 8 feet high, spreading about 10 feet wide. Plant them about 10 to 15 feet apart. Cut the top back to about 2 ½ feet tall. Water regularly, avoiding high-nitrogen fertilizer. Feed in the spring, using a commercial fertilizer such as a 10–10–10 formula. Thin the branches regularly, letting light in from the top, and thin the fruit to 3 to 4 inches apart when it reaches about ¾ inch in diameter.

The apricot tree should start producing fruit in 3 to 4 years. Harvest when the fruit is ripe and can be picked easily.

BLACKBERRIES: See RASPBERRIES

BLUEBERRIES: Blueberries are hardy shrubs that work well for landscaping as well as producing fruit. The most common variety is the highbush blueberry, which can grow 8 to 10 feet tall if not pruned. Blueberries do best in full sun, good air circulation, and moist but not wet soil. The soil should be loose and contain plenty of acidic organic matter such as peat moss.

It is best to buy dormant plants 2 to 3 years old, keeping the roots moist until planting. Plant in early spring in holes about 1½ feet wide and deep. Plant highbush blueberries about 6 feet apart if you are interested primarily in the fruit, 3 feet apart if you want a hedge. Keep the plants moist, particularly during the first year, and fertilize well when they blossom, using a high-acid commercial fertilizer. Avoid excessive nitrogen. After about 4 years, prune annually when the plants are dormant.

For the first few years, berries should be rubbed off to encourage plant growth. When the plant starts to produce, harvest the fruit once or twice a week. Hold your hand under the berry cluster and rub the berries with your thumb. The ripe berries will fall into your hand. Don't pull any off that don't fall off easily.

BOYSENBERRIES: See RASPBERRIES

CHERRIES: There are two basic varieties of cherries, sweet cherries for eating and sour cherries for cooking.

Sour cherries are hardier and easier to grow. The trees grow up to about 15 feet, while sweet cherry trees grow to about 25 feet. Sour cherry trees should be planted about 20 feet apart, and sweet cherries about 30 to 40 feet. Most varieties require a different variety growing nearby to ensure cross-pollination. Check with your local nursery to see which types do best in your area.

Cherry trees do best in full sun and well-drained, slightly sandy soil. It is best to buy 1-to-2-year-old dormant trees, cutting them back before planting. Apply mulch around the roots, particularly if planting in the fall. Water the trees deeply, particularly when they bloom and when the fruit ripens. Feed in the early spring with a balanced commercial fertilizer such as a 10–10–10 formula. Prune regularly to let light in from the top.

Harvest the fruit when it looks ripe and is easily picked, leaving the stems on the fruit. Sweet cherries will keep a week or two in the refrigerator. Sour cherries should be used right away.

CITRUS: Lemons, limes, oranges, and grapefruit vary somewhat in hardiness, but generally prefer warm to hot climates. Limes cannot tolerate any frost, while grapefruit and oranges can survive occasional temperatures in the 20s. Lemons and limes bloom and produce fruit year round, while oranges and grapefruit are spring bloomers, going dormant in winter.

Citrus trees prefer full sun and plenty of heat. The exception would be desert regions, where partial shade is better. Moist but well-drained soil is best. Most citrus trees are grafted. Plant with the graft about 6 inches aboveground, keeping the soil moist, particularly during the first year. The roots tend to be shallow and wide, so water accordingly. Top-feed regularly with a fertilizer rich in nitrogen. Keep the area around the tree free of weeds and even grass. Citrus trees usually don't require pruning.

Lemons, limes, and some oranges, such as Valencias, can be picked all year. Other oranges and grapefruit are harvested in winter and spring. Citrus fruit must be fully ripened before picking. The best way to tell is to pick one and taste it.

GRAPEFRUIT: See **CITRUS**

GRAPES: Grapes need full sun and good air circulation. Most are self-pollinating. Check with your local nursery for the types that do best in your area, and for compatible varieties where cross-pollination is necessary. Since grapes are wind-pollinated, they need to be planted within 40 to 50 feet of one another.

Grapes can grow in most any kind of soil, but do best in slightly sandy, well-drained soil with plenty of organic matter. Get 1-year-old plants from your nursery and plant them while dormant in the early spring. Cut back the top of the plant so that only two nodes remain. The vines will have to be supported, and it is easier to plan and install a support system, such as a trellis, when planting. Plant about 8 feet apart, in a hole about a foot deep and wide, adding moist peat.

Grapes require little water or fertilizer, although a little nitrogen-based fertilizer will help. Train the vines to grow on the support as soon as possible. Prune the plant so that you have a few lateral vines growing out from the main trunk, letting the plant add a new lateral vine or two every year. Train the laterals to grow out along horizontal support vines or arms on the trellis.

Grapes must fully ripen on the vine before being harvested. Go by taste rather than looks in deciding when to harvest.

LEMONS: See **CITRUS**

LIMES: See **CITRUS**

LOGANBERRIES: See **RASPBERRIES**

NECTARINES: See **PEACHES**

ORANGES: See **CITRUS**

PEACHES: Peaches and nectarines are basically the same fruit. Peaches have fuzzy skin, while nectarine skin is smooth. Some peaches are self-pollinating, so you can get fruit from a single tree, but most require another variety nearby for cross-pollination. Most varieties will not tolerate winter temperatures below zero. Peaches grow best on a slope above a body of water. They require full sun and very good drainage. They prefer light, sandy soil that drains well and warms up quickly.

Buy 1-year-old trees and plant them in the early spring when they are dormant. Plant dwarfs about 10 feet apart, full-size trees about 20 feet apart. Plant with the graft aboveground and cut the tree back to about 3 feet tall.

Top-feed lightly in spring and in early summer with a balanced commercial fertilizer such as a 10–10–10 formula. Prune annually when the tree is dormant. Allow 3 or 4 strong main branches, avoiding a central leader or trunk. The fruit should be thinned to about 6 inches apart so that each peach has about 35 to 40 leaves supporting it. Harvest the fruit when the peach loses its green color.

PEARS: Pear trees grow up to 25 feet high, producing fruit for 50 to 75 years. They are sturdier than peach trees and require a cold winter for dormancy. Pears must cross-pollinate, and several varieties are not compatible. Check with your local nursery to see what grows well in your area and which are compatible.

Pears prefer full sun except in very hot climates and need good air circulation. They require deep, preferably heavy soil with a lot of moisture.

Plant pears in early spring, buying 1-to-2-year-old trees that you cut back to about 3 feet high after planting. Add organic matter, avoiding nitrogen. With dwarfs, make sure that the graft is planted several inches aboveground.

Make sure that the soil is kept moist. Little feeding is generally required, but if the foliage is pale, top-feed with a balanced commercial fertilizer, such as a 10–10–10 formula. It is best to underfeed pear trees to avoid diseases. Prune regularly, making sure that light can come in from the top.

It is best to pick pears before they ripen on the tree. Pick them when the skin is light green and the seeds inside are brown. Store in a dry place that is as cool as possible without the risk of freezing.

PERSIMMONS: Persimmon trees grow 20 to 30 feet high, and their leaves turn brilliant reds and yellows in the fall. For best results, buy plants 1 to 2 years old. Set out potted trees at any time. Bare-root plants should be planted in the early spring as soon as the ground can be worked. At planting, prune off all but 4 or 5 good branches. Feed at the beginning of the second spring with a balanced commercial fertilizer such as a 10–10–10 formula. Thin out the fruit so that the persimmons are about 6 inches apart. Harvest when the fruit is soft by snipping the stems with shears.

PLUMS: Plums grow on small trees and are self-pollinating. They do better, however, if allowed to cross-pollinate with another variety of the same basic color group. Check with your nursery to see which varieties are best for cross-pollination in your area.

Plums will tolerate a wide range of conditions, but do best in full sun and deep, well-drained soil with plenty of organic matter. Plant year-old trees in early spring while they are still dormant. Water regularly and top-feed annually with a balanced commercial fertilizer. Prune occasionally to let light into the center of the tree.

The fruit is ripe when it comes off the branch with a little twist. Red plums should not be picked until fully ripened. Blue plums can be picked a little early and left to ripen off the tree.

RASPBERRIES: The family of berries known by the scientific name *rubus* includes raspberries, blackberries, loganberries, boysenberries, and youngberries. They are also known as bramble fruit. These are perennial plants that produce fruit on biennial canes. The plant lives on from year to year, sending out canes that bear fruit in 2 years and then die. The dead canes should be removed regularly to allow new growth.

Blackberries are larger than raspberries and not as sweet. They do better in warmer climates. Boysenberries and loganberries are varieties of blackberry.

These plants do best in full sun, with a slight slope for drainage. Any wild berries in the immediate area should be removed, as they can transmit disease. These berries do best in slightly acid soil with plenty of organic matter. They are very disease prone, and should only be grown from nursery certified virus-free plants.

Plant in the early spring, placing the plants about 3 feet apart. Keep the roots moist and cut the plants back to about 6 inches tall. Keep the soil moist throughout the growing season, and top-feed with a balanced commercial fertilizer such as a 5–10–5 formula in the spring. A trellis can be used to make the berries easier to pick and to keep the plants from taking up too much space.

Berries should not be picked until they are fully ripe. They should be picked a couple of times a week when they are ripening, taking care to pull the berries off the stem without squeezing. Don't let them get too deep in your container or they will be squashed. After harvesting, cut back all fruit-bearing canes to ground level.

STRAWBERRIES: Strawberries require regular care to prevent bugs, weeds, and diseases, although they are hardy perennials that grow well on their own.

There are four kinds of strawberries. The classic berry bears a lot of fruit for a few weeks and then is through for the year. So-called ever-bearing strawberries produce 2 crops, one in late spring, the other in late summer. The crops are smaller than the classic type, and the plants less hardy.

Day-neutral strawberries produce steadily throughout the summer. Alpine strawberries produce a very small crop throughout the season.

Strawberries require full sun and well-drained soil. The soil should be fertile with plenty of organic matter, and must be kept completely free of weeds. Plant in the early spring, buying from a local nursery that can certify the plants as disease free. Dig a hole, leaving a cone of dirt pointing up in the middle of the hole. Place the plant on the point of the cone with the roots draping down into the hole. Make sure that the crown of the plant, where the roots come together, is exactly at soil level.

The first year, any flowers should be pinched off. Top-feed annually when the plants blossom, using a balanced commercial fertilizer. The plants send out runners that go out about 9 inches and send down roots, becoming new plants. You will have to thin out these runners, both to give yourself room to walk between the rows and to keep the plants from becoming a tangled mess.

Strawberries should be fully ripened before picking. Wait until the berry is completely red. Pinch the berries off at the stem, taking care not to touch the fruit itself. Collect in shallow containers, or the weight will crush the berries at the bottom.

YOUNGBERRIES: See RASPBERRIES

9

SHRUBS AND EVERGREENS

Shrub is a fairly general term referring to small woody plants with many stems. The distinction between big shrubs and small trees is often blurred. Shrubs include both deciduous plants and evergreens. Shrubs may have needles, leaves, flowers, and/or berries. Shrubs are traditionally used as a border around walks, lawns, entrances, or gardens. They are also used as hedges, forming a living fence around property.

Evergreen is also a pretty general term, referring to any plant that remains green through the winter, particularly in colder climates. Most people tend to think of the smaller-needled evergreens such as juniper when the term is used. But there are also broad-leaved evergreens, some of which bear flowers.

There are dozens if not hundreds of shrubs commonly grown in this country. They vary widely in their ability to grow in different conditions, whether sun or shade, heat or cold, dryness or moisture. Given the relatively high cost of shrubs, as compared with flowers or vegetables, some local research is particularly important before buying plants.

In colder climates, shrubs should usually be planted in early spring while the plants are still dormant. Some shrubs, such as needled evergreens, can be planted in the fall even in the north. In warmer climates, shrubs should be planted in fall or winter, allowing them to get well established before the stress of a hot summer. Bare-root shrubs should be planted in spring, while others are hardier and more flexible as to time of planting.

Individual shrubs should be planted far enough apart so that they don't intrude on one another. Remember that most shrubs will be about as wide as they are tall. Height estimates are available for most plants, so plan accordingly. If you are planting for hedges, plant about 2 to 3 feet apart.

Most shrubs need to be pruned regularly for various reasons. New shrubs should be cut back to compensate for root loss during transplanting. Pruning also encourages growth. Pruning the terminal bud from the end of a twig or branch allows the side buds on that stem to increase leaf production greatly. Shrubs are also pruned to attain the desired height or shape. Remember that when you cut back to a bud on the branch, new growth will be in the direction that bud is facing, whether in or out, up or down.

Older shrubs can be greatly improved by careful pruning. Cut back long leggy branches, excessive main stems, or just plain too much growth. Major thinning is best done in late winter or early spring when the shrub is dormant. If you are pruning to control excessive growth, do it in late summer. Take particular care in pruning flowering shrubs. Some shrubs produce flowers on new growth, twigs or branches that have grown the same year. These bloom late in the season and should be pruned in late winter or early spring. Other shrubs produce flowers on old wood that grew the year before. These bloom early in the year and should be pruned right after blooming.

Shrubs and evergreens are usually purchased as well-developed plants, either growing in containers or with their roots wrapped in a ball of burlap. A balled and burlapped plant should have a tight wrap, and the soil should be the soil the plant originally grew in. Container-grown plants should be checked to see that the root system is not over-grown and constricted.

Plant by digging a hole twice the diameter of the root ball or container and about 1½ times as deep. Mix the dug-up soil with peat moss, and add peat moss to the bottom of the hole. For a plant in a container, moisten the soil and remove the plant from the container. If the container is plastic, turn it on its side and tap the plant out, taking care not to pull it by the trunk. If the container is fiber, slit it with a heavy sharp knife. Loosen any roots around the outside of the root ball. Put enough soil and peat-moss mixture back into the hole so that the plant will sit with the top of its root ball at ground level. If the plant is wrapped in burlap, put the whole thing in the hole as above. Fill the hole until about half of the root ball is covered with soil. Then cut loose the burlap and pull it down away from the root ball.

Fill in the hole, building a watering basin around the plant with a ridge of soil. If the plant is tall, you may want to anchor it with some guy lines, particularly if it is in a very windy place. Do not feed a newly transplanted evergreen until it is well established, but do give it plenty of water.

TYPES OF SHRUBS AND EVERGREENS

AZALEA: Azaleas can be either deciduous or evergreen, and all are members of the rhododendron family. They vary greatly in size, with some growing up to 12 feet high. Different varieties bloom from spring to late summer, and the flowers come in a wide range of color. See the section on rhododendrons for general growing information.

Azaleas should be pruned when young to encourage growth, and the tips should be pinched to increase blooming.

BARBERRY: Barberry grows wild in some areas, producing tiny yellow flowers that look like roses. In the fall, the shrub produces bright red berries. It is thorny and may appear weedy, but can be used as a hedge. Barberry grows in most soils, and requires little water. It will grow well in sun or shade.

BURNING BUSH: See **EUONYMUS**

CAMELLIA: Camellias can't be grown in cooler climates, but they bloom in the winter in the south. There are hundreds of varieties of camellia, with flowers 2 to 4 inches across and glossy evergreen leaves. They need protection from wind and direct hot sun. Water well, particularly when the plants are young. Prune after blooming to just above this season's growth.

CEDAR: There are many trees referred to as cedar, but only 3 true cedars grow in this country. These are the Atlas cedar, deodar cedar, and cedar of Lebanon. They all have 1-to-2-inch needles that grow in clusters of 6 to 12 along the branches. They do best in full sun and well-drained soil. They are difficult to transplant, particularly if balled and burlapped.

COLORADO FIR: See **WHITE FIR**

EUONYMUS: This shrub has deciduous and evergreen varieties, which are very different from one another. One variety, called burning bush or spindle tree, grows treelike as it gets old. It turns red in the fall, with red berries. Burning bush requires little water once established, and does not need much pruning. Evergreen varieties grow up to 4 feet high and may need 1 or 2 prunings a year to control growth and shape.

FORSYTHIA: Forsythia grows in a big mound with long stems. It will grow in most conditions, but does best in moist soil. Prune after blooming, since the flowers grow on the previous year's growth. Excessive pruning tends to ruin the flower growth. Planted 5 to 6 feet apart, forsythia will grow into a dense hedge.

HEMLOCK: Hemlock is a tall, narrow evergreen, growing to 25 feet and more if not pruned. They do well as single trees or as screens, and can be easily sheared into hedges. Hemlock grows best in cool areas, in moist soil and full sun or partial shade. It generally does not do well in the city, or on dry windy plains. Hemlocks rarely require feeding, and can be pruned or sheared at will.

HONEYSUCKLE: Honeysuckle grows as a vine and as a shrub. The shrub produces fragrant spring flowers followed by red berries. They can grow up to 9 feet high. Winter honeysuckle is compact and is an evergreen in warmer climates. Honeysuckle will tolerate partial shade, but does best in full sun and moist soil. It requires a minimum of pruning, removing only dead wood or very weak growth. Prune in early spring, since honeysuckle shrubs bloom on new wood.

HYDRANGEA: Hydrangea produces a lot of large flowers in the middle of summer. The flowers can be left on the plant to dry for bouquets. Most hydrangeas have an unusual characteristic of producing pink flowers in alkaline soil and blue flowers in acid soil. Hydrangeas do best in fertile soil with plenty of organic matter. The soil should be moist but well drained. They do not require a lot of watering. Prune after blooming.

JUNIPER: Most junipers are shrublike, although some, like red cedar, are trees. They tolerate poor soil and can grow in hot dry places. They grow in a wide variety of shapes and colors. Some grow tall in a cone shape, while others are low and spreading. Dwarf varieties can be grown in rock gardens or in containers. Junipers do best in full sun and dry sandy soil. They do not require much feeding or pruning, although they do respond well to trimming.

LILAC: Lilacs are very hardy plants with fragrant flowers, but usually with tall and leggy shrubs. Best known for their lavender color, they also grow in purple, red, and white. They prefer a light, well-drained soil, neutral rather than acid. Prune only after the plants have become well established. Pinch off old flowers after they fade.

OLEANDER: This plant grows best in the south, producing large flowers in a variety of colors. The leaves are evergreen, and oleanders can be trained to grow treelike up to 20 feet high. The plants are poisonous to people and animals. Oleander prefers full sun and soil with good drainage. Cutting off fading flowers will encourage further blooming. An old plant can be rejuvenated by cutting it back to about 6 inches high.

PINE: There are dozens of varieties of pine, with 40 or 50 native to North America. Most have broad conical shapes when young, rounding out on top as they grow older. The needles grow in bundles of 2 to 5, wrapped at the base with a papery sheath. Pines require full sun and do best in well-drained but average soil. They do not require fertilizer or any particular soil preparation when planting. Pruning will make them short and bushy.

PRIVET: Privet is best known as a hedge plant. It is easily trimmed, and the trimming encourages quick and dense growth. Privet turns green early in the spring and stays so late into fall. Some varieties are evergreen. They grow well in most soils, but do need good drainage. They will grow in full sun or partial shade. Plant about 1 to 2 feet apart to form a solid hedge. Shear the hedge in early spring and again in early summer.

RHODODENDRON: Rhododendron includes hundreds of varieties, including azaleas. Check with your local nursery to see which types do best in your area. The foliage is usually evergreen, and the plant produces exceptional flower clusters. They grow tall, with some varieties growing up to 15 feet high or more. They prefer a light moist soil with plenty of organic matter, but don't need very deep soil preparation. They do best if protected from strong winds or direct sunlight in winter. They should be planted in early spring in the north, early fall in the south. They require little in the way of pruning or feeding. Pinch off fading flowers just above the new buds to encourage further growth. Cut back overgrown plants in the early spring.

SPRUCE: Spruce are evergreen trees with the classic Christmas-tree shape. They grow fairly slowly and are useful garden plants when young, although they might eventually have to be removed. They do best in full sun and prefer moist soil. They can tolerate drier areas if they are watered frequently until they become well established. They require little pruning, being naturally symmetrical.

WHITE FIR: White or Colorado firs grow in dense, perfectly conical shapes when young, although the lower part of the plant thins with age and they lose their shape. These firs bear their seeds in pine cones along the higher branches. They do not do well in hot dry climates and don't tolerate polluted air. They do best in full sun and require little pruning.

YEW: Yew is an evergreen that is used widely for hedges. Most varieties are trees, but there are some compact types that grow well as hedges. The larger ones can also be pruned into hedges. They produce bright red berries that are poisonous. Yews grow in full sun or partial shade and prefer moist but well-drained soil. They need to be well watered before winter sets in. They can be lightly sheared at any time, but heavy pruning should be done in early spring before the season's new growth starts.

10

TREES

Fruit trees and evergreens have been discussed in other chapters. That still leaves an extremely wide range of trees to talk about. The home gardener generally thinks of trees in terms of planting a few for ornamental purposes. Thus the main consideration is how a particular type of tree will look in a particular place. It is also necessary to think about how it will look some years down the road, since it is going to be rather small and thin for some time to come. In considering trees for your property, it is much better to visit a park or a botanical garden than a nursery so that you can see what the tree will look like for the major portion of its life. The nursery, however, will be a good source of information about what trees grow well in your area and how to grow them.

While appearance is the major consideration in planting a tree, there are some other things to think about. One thing to keep in mind is that a large deciduous tree close to the house can be a good source of shade during the summer. Trees can also provide privacy, cut down on wind, and even prevent heavy snowdrifting.

In addition to the general climate of the area, there are many other conditions to consider in choosing a tree for your yard. If you live in the city, you may need a tree that can tolerate soot, smog, and other pollutants. The spot where you will plant the tree may be in full sun, or it may be shaded by buildings or other trees. The particular spot you have in mind may have very good or very poor drainage.

One more important thing to keep in mind when planting a tree, particularly in the city, is where the top of the tree is going to be in 10 or 20 years. You can see where the power lines and phone lines are. Don't plant a tree within 15 to 20 feet of these lines. You can't see where the sewer lines or water pipes or buried cables are, but it is a good idea to find out. Just call your local utility company, tell them that you need locator service, and they will come out and mark their right-of-way. If you don't, you and your tree could be in trouble some years hence.

When buying a tree, remember that the younger the tree is, the easier it is to transplant and establish. In addition, smaller trees are simply easier to work with. And younger trees are less expensive than older, larger ones, both in terms of buying the tree and in the cost of the labor to transplant it. These factors are offset by the pleasure of having a full-grown or nearly full-grown tree transplanted and in place immediately.

BUYING AND PLANTING

It is best to buy a tree from a reputable nursery. If you buy a few pots of annual flowers from the supermarket and they don't do very well, you can start over next spring. A poor-quality tree could grow for several years before showing signs of problems.

Watch out for trees with yellowed or wilted leaves. Look for a small tree with good shape and a few strong branches. Check the root system if it is in a pot to make sure that it is not root bound, with the roots cramped and crawling out of the pot. Balled and burlapped trees should have a tight, moist root ball with no obvious damage.

Most trees will come with their roots in a ball of dirt wrapped in burlap. To plant, dig a hole about twice the diameter of the root ball and half again as deep. Work some peat moss into the soil that you dug out of the hole. Build a mound of dirt in the bottom of the hole that will position the tree so that the top of the root ball is at ground level. Fill the hole until just over half of the root ball is covered. Untie or slice the burlap and peel it down to uncover the top half of the root ball. Continue to fill in the hole, tamping down the dirt to ensure that there are no air pockets. Make a circular ridge of dirt around the trunk of the tree, forming a watering basin that will allow water to soak deep into the roots.

A young tree may have to be supported until it is well established, particularly in a windy place. One way to do this is to drive a pair of tall 2 x 4 stakes into the ground on opposite sides of the tree and attach the tree to the stakes with heavy wire threaded through lengths of garden hose to protect the tree trunk. An alternate method is to sink 3 or 4 short 2 x 4 stakes into the ground around the tree and run guy wires from the tree to the stakes. Again, the part of the wire that actually touches the trees should be passed through a length of garden hose to protect the bark of the tree trunk.

Newly planted trees should not be fed for several weeks. Feed the tree for the first time after planting in the early fall, using a dry commercial fertilizer such as 10–10–10. After that, feed it in early spring with a garden fertilizer, such as 5–10–5. Well-established trees generally do not require any special feeding, but occasional fertilizing will help keep them healthy. A good commercial tree fertilizer is a 10–8–6 formula, but a good lawn fertilizer usually works just as well.

Early spring is generally the best time for pruning. Remove any dead wood and trim off any branches that grow in toward the middle of the tree, or any that grow straight up or straight down. Prune so that there is a single leader or central trunk, and keep the central portion of the tree thinned out so that sunlight can reach all parts of the tree.

Young trees should be watered regularly, about once a week. It is better to give the tree a deep soaking once a week than to water it lightly every day or two. Light sprinkling will cause the root system to be very shallow. Well-established trees generally do not require watering except in drought conditions.

COMMON TREES

ASH: White ash grows very quickly and very tall, up to 120 feet. Other varieties, such as the green ash, are smaller. The trees produce dappled shade, and their fall foliage is colorful. Ash trees are easy to grow, preferring full sun and moist, rich soil. The wood tends to be fragile, so it is important to prune the weaker branches.

BEECH: Beeches have large, round heads of foliage, creating deep shade where little else will grow. Beech leaves turn dark gold in fall, and the gray bark is beautiful in winter. Its shallow roots often emerge from the ground, radiating out from the trunk. American beech can grow up to 80 feet high and 50 feet wide. Beech prefers well-drained, acid soil with plenty of organic matter. They prefer full sun, but will tolerate partial shade. They are best planted balled and burlapped, and should not be planted too deeply, as the roots grow shallow.

BIRCH: Birches have open branches that give light shade. They are fast growing, but do not live long. The most familiar variety is the paper or canoe birch, with white bark marked with black bands. The bark is usually brown for the first few years, turning white as the tree matures. Birches can grow up to 80 feet high. Birches tend to grow in clumps, but will live longer if pruned to a single trunk. Birches are best planted balled and burlapped. They need full sun and moist but well-drained soil. It is best to prune them while they are young, before the sap begins to flow in late winter. Birches pruned in early spring usually bleed excessively.

BOX ELDER: See **MAPLE**

DOGWOOD: The flowering dogwood is the most familiar variety and will grow in most areas. They grow 25 to 30 feet high, with horizontal branches. Planted when 6 feet high, they will grow to about 15 feet in 5 years. They produce small white or pink flowers, and the leaves turn dark red in fall. There are several varieties of dogwood, including some that are very shrubby. Dogwoods prefer full sun and moist, well-drained soil, slightly acid, with plenty of organic matter. Plant dogwood balled and burlapped in the early spring. Flowering dogwood should not be pruned unless absolutely necessary. It tends to bleed, and heals slowly.

HAWTHORN: Hawthorns are small ornamental trees that produce clusters of small, white flowers in the spring and red berries in the fall. There are hundreds of varieties, mostly native to North America, and they are very easy to grow. They do have thorns, and grow from 15 to 30 feet high, depending on type. They are best planted when small, as they are very hard to move once established. Plant balled and burlapped in the early spring. Hawthorns have long taproots and should be transplanted while still small, no more than 8 feet high. They prefer full sun and will tolerate drought and poor soil, either acid or alkaline. Prune in the very early spring while the tree is still dormant, removing center branches to let sunlight in.

LARCH: Larches look like evergreens, with needlelike leaves that turn yellow and fall off in autumn. Larch is fast growing and hardy, growing up to 90 feet high. Larches require a cool climate, but prefer full sun and deep rich soil, moist, well drained, and slightly acid. It is best to plant them balled and burlapped in the fall or early spring. They rarely need to be pruned.

LINDEN: Lindens are fast-growing shade trees, widely used in Europe to line city streets. They produce clusters of white flowers in midsummer. Lindens grow best in deep, rich soil, moist but well drained. They do well in full sun or partial shade. They should be planted balled and burlapped, and should be pruned in late winter to form a single strong trunk. Older trees should be thinned regularly.

MAGNOLIA: Magnolias are generally thought of as southern trees, but some species can be grown in most parts of the north. The most common type, the saucer magnolia, grows to about 25 feet high with large purple flowers and dark gray bark. They need full sun, except in the north, where they should be planted in partial shade to discourage early blooming. Magnolias grow best in loose, well-drained soil that is slightly acid and has plenty of organic matter. Dead or diseased wood should be removed, but otherwise do not prune magnolias.

MAPLE: There are many varieties of maple, ranging from the Japanese maple, which grows to about 25 feet, to the sugar maple, which can reach over 100 feet high. They are grown by gardeners for shade and for ornamentation. Varieties include sycamore and box elder. Some varieties, such as sycamore maples, grow very fast. An 8-foot-high young planting can grow to 20 feet within 5 to 6 years. Sugar maple, on the other hand, grows very slowly, taking about 8 years to reach 20 feet. Maples produce bright fall colors and winged seeds that spin down when dropped. They are easy to grow and do best in moist soil with full sun. They require cool winters to produce their bright fall colors. Maples should be pruned in early fall when the sap is not running.

MIMOSA: Mimosas are generally grown in the south. They grow up to 40 feet high, with fuzzy pink flowers in the summer followed by long dangling seed pods. They are short-lived, usually lasting only about 30 years. They do best in full sun, but will tolerate partial shade, and require well-drained soil. They should be planted balled and burlapped when young. Plant in the early spring, and prune to a single trunk if desired.

MULBERRY: The mulberry is a tough, versatile tree that can take the bad air of the city and can also tolerate heat and drought. It will reach its full height of 30 to 40 feet in 8 to 10 years. Mulberries generally have several trunks, which become twisted with age. They prefer full sun, and will grow in any soil, even highly alkaline.

OAK: Oaks are sturdy, long-lived trees that grow up to 100 feet high. All varieties produce acorns, and some retain their dead leaves through the fall. Oaks prefer full sun and slightly acid soil. They can be pruned while young to produce a strong central leader and to develop longer branches. They generally do not need pruning once well established.

PECAN: Pecan trees need long, hot summers to produce their nuts. They grow slowly, but can eventually reach over 100 feet high. They usually take about 5 to 6 years to produce nuts. Pecans need full sun and moist soil. They are easiest to plant bare-root when very young. Their long deep roots make them difficult to transplant. They rarely need pruning.

POPLAR: Poplars are fast-growing, beautiful trees whose roots have a tendency to heave sidewalks and wreck plumbing. They will average about 4 feet of growth a year, growing from 50 to 100 feet high depending on type. They grow in most areas, preferring full sun and well-drained, deep soil. They should be pruned in the summer or fall, or they will bleed.

SWEET GUM: Sweet gum trees are a good choice for shade trees to be planted along city streets. They grow best in moist soil, reaching up to 30 feet in 7 to 8 years. Growth is much slower if the soil is dry. They will eventually reach up to 70 feet high. They grow best in full sun and moist soil with plenty of organic matter. They are best planted balled and burlapped in the spring. Sweet gums should be pruned in the winter.

SYCAMORE: See **MAPLE**

WALNUT: Walnuts are grown as shade trees as well as for their nuts. They are fast growing, and should be planted when 3 to 4 feet high. They will grow to about 20 feet in 6 to 7 years. For good nut production, two or more must be planted together for cross-pollination. Walnuts require full sun and deep, well-drained soil. Plant bare-rooted trees in the early spring. Prune in late summer or early fall. Spring pruning results in bleeding.

WILLOW: Weeping willow is the best-known species. It is best planted by a stream or pond and away from plumbing, which can be wrecked by its roots. Willows grow in most soils, but do best in moist or even wet soil. They should be watered regularly until well established. They prefer full sun. They are generally very easy to grow and can be planted bare-root. Prune the tree while young to establish a central trunk.

11

LAWNS

The terms *lawn* and *grass* are often used interchangeably. A lawn is a ground cover of green vegetation and is usually made of grass. In certain locations, ground covers of something other than grass are more common, because of local growing conditions or preferences. Grasses are particularly good for ground covers for a number of reasons. For one thing, grasses grow from the bottom up. Since new growth appears at the bottom of the leaf, mowing removes older growth and does not affect the plant. For another, you can walk on grass. Few other ground covers can be walked on without damage.

There are many varieties of grasses used for lawns in this country, with varying characteristics of growth rate, preference for sunlight, watering needs, and so on. The most practical method is to plant a mixture of several types of grass. This makes the lawn less vulnerable to disease and allows the grasses to find their ideal locations in a lawn with varying conditions. One type will flourish in areas that get full sun, while another will do well in a shady corner on the north side of the house. In picking a mixture, check to see what varieties of grass are included. Certain types, such as rye grass, may be included because they sprout quickly and produce quick results. These grasses may take water and nutrients from the other types in the mixture that normally come up later and are intended to be the long-term permanent lawn.

Selecting the right mixture is more of a problem in the north, where lawns are typically started from seed. In the south, grass is usually grown from living plants that propagate by sending out lateral stems that take root. Lawns in the south are more likely to be a single type of grass. The most popular species are Bermuda, zoysia, St. Augustine, and centipede. Bermuda is the most popular, largely because it spreads very quickly. St. Augustine and centipede grasses are grown in the deep south, particularly along the Gulf Coast. Neither tolerates cold weather, and St. Augustine can survive salt air and spray.

LAWN CARE

Ideally, the first step in caring for your lawn should be taken before planting. That is to determine whether the soil is acid or alkaline. Either test the soil yourself with a home testing kit or take a soil sample to a testing lab, such as at an agricultural college. Take the soil sample below ground, at the grass root level. After you know the acidity or alkalinity of the soil, you can either select the best grass for your soil or change the chemical condition of your soil to suit the grass you want to plant. For example, centipede grass does well in acid soil, while buffalo grass can survive in very alkaline soil. Excess acidity can be corrected through an application of lime, while excess alkalinity is offset by adding sulfur. Adding either will also help break up soil with a high clay content.

Lawn fertilizer should contain the three major nutrients: nitrogen, phosphorus, and potassium. Nitrogen is the most important nutrient for grass, and one that tends to wash out of the soil easily. Therefore lawn fertilizers should be high in nitrogen. A typical grass fertilizer would be a 10–6–4 formula. The need for other nutrients can vary from one region to another. For example, the soil in southern coastal states tends to be low in phosphorus, and lawn fertilizers used there will usually contain more of that nutrient than normal. Soil in the east is more likely to need additional potassium than in the west.

There are three types of lawn fertilizers, and they must be used differently. Inorganic fertilizers contain chemical salts that can burn grass. They should be applied in the early spring when the grass is very dry, but not when the grass is dried out from drought. Organic fertilizers are made from organic matter such as manure or plant material. They are very slow acting, since they must decay to release their nutrients. They should be applied in the spring so that they can work through the hot, humid weather of summer when they decay best. Synthetic organic fertilizers, the third type, also release their nutrients very slowly.

Grasses should be fertilized just before they begin their most active growth period. For cool-climate grasses grown in the north, this usually means that they should be fed in the early spring and again in the early fall. Hot-weather grasses need to be fed in early spring and again in mid-summer. The best and easiest way to apply fertilizer is with a spreader. Read the instructions for the spreader and those on the fertilizer to ensure proper application. Make sure that your spreader is thoroughly cleaned after use, or it will be corroded by leftover fertilizer.

Lawns need to be watered regularly, but just how often varies with your area and current weather conditions. It is much better to water a lawn deeply every 2 to 3 days than to water it lightly every day. Deep watering lets the water soak into the ground where it will not evaporate as quickly, and it encourages good root growth. Use some kind of sprinkler watering device and avoid watering at the hottest times of day or when it is very windy. Hot sun and strong winds will evaporate quite a bit of the water spray before it gets down to the ground. The best time to water is in the morning before the sun gets hot. Watering in the evening can cause certain grass diseases.

A good healthy lawn is its own best protection against weeds. A thick cover of grass will keep the sunlight from reaching weeds and thus keep them from sprouting. During the peak weed-growth season, set the lawn mower height a little higher so that less sun reaches down through the grass. Many grasses should be allowed to grow an additional ½ inch to a full inch higher in hot weather. Regular mowing also cuts off the tops of weeds before they can go to seed.

If weeds do get established, you may have to use a chemical weed killer. There are two basic kinds, one for broad-leaf weeds and one for grassy weeds. Broad-leaf weeds, such as dandelions, can be killed with a specifically designed chemical such as 2, 4-D. This is actually a hormone compound, which speeds up the weed growth so fast that the weed wears out and dies. This kind of weed killer is sprayed directly on the individual weed. Check first to see that your grass will tolerate the weed killer you want to use. Bent grass, for one, will be damaged by 2, 4-D. The most common kind of grassy weed is crabgrass. There are two types of treatment for crabgrass: preemergent and postemergent. The first is designed to kill seedlings and is usually applied only once a season in the spring. The second kills established plants and may require repeated applications. There are various types of grassy weed killers. Again, make sure that your species of grass can tolerate a specific weed killer before using it.

For the most part, you should not have to worry too much about pests in the lawn. Regular care, including mowing, watering, feeding, and particularly dethatching, will keep the lawn healthy enough that pests will not be a problem. If you do have pests bad enough to cause bare spots, check with your local nursery to see what you have and what to do about it.

MOWING

There are two basic types of lawn mowers: the rotary mower and the reel mower. The rotary mower generally has a single blade, set parallel to the ground and spun at high speed by a gas or electric motor. The spinning blade is sharpened at the ends and clips off the grass as it whirls through it. Even a dull rotary blade will cut grass, but it also bruises the ends of the blades and could turn the grass brown. Rotary mowers are usually less expensive and easier to use than reel mowers and are thus much more common.

A reel mower has a series of spiral blades mounted across a stationary metal bar. The grass is cut in a scissorslike action as the grass passes between the spinning reel blades and the stationary bar. The lawn is cut smoother as the reel spins faster, and a reel with more blades cuts better and smoother than one with fewer blades. Reel mowers can be adjusted much more precisely than rotary models, and it is reel mowers that are generally used by such professionals as golf-course grounds keepers.

Don't mow the grass when it is wet, or even damp, from rain or watering. Always mow before feeding or seeding a lawn, and never mow within 24 hours after feeding or seeding. Change your mowing pattern from one mowing to the next. Maintain the recommended height for the type of grass in your lawn. The grass should be higher in hot weather, particularly in drought conditions, and shorter when the weather is cooler. The grass should be cut as low as possible for the last mowing of the fall, and make sure to pick up the clippings.

LAWN MAINTENANCE

There are a couple of major lawn-care chores that should be done fairly regularly and that have to be done if the lawn is not growing properly. These are aerating and dethatching.

Aerating opens up heavily compacted soil, allowing air, water, and nutrients to reach the root system more easily. Aerating is particularly important for soil that contains a lot of clay. Aerating consists of either poking holes in the ground or of extracting thin plugs of dirt from the ground. It can be done with a spiking machine, which has spikes on a roller. An easier and more efficient way to aerate a lawn is with a power aerator. This machine has a rotating drum with hollow tubes sticking out. As the drum turns, the tubes are forced into the ground and each extracts a round plug of dirt. Aerators can be rented from nurseries or equipment rental firms.

Thatch is a dense layer of stems, grass clippings, and other organic matter that builds up on the lawn. If this organic matter builds up faster than it can decompose, it can prevent water, air, and fertilizer from reaching the grass. Thatch also is a breeding ground for diseases and bugs. As a matter of routine maintenance, your lawn should be dethatched at least every other year. An optimal schedule is to dethatch in early spring and again in the early fall, every year. Thatch can be removed with a dethatcher rake, but this requires a lot of effort and can seriously damage a lawn. It is easier and safer to rent a dethatching machine, a lawn-mower-like device especially designed to remove thatch. The job should be done in the early spring or in the early fall. If you have a compost heap, the thatch you remove from your lawn is an excellent composting material.

Bare spots should be replanted with plugs or with seeds, depending on the type of grass you are planting. If there are just some thin spots in the lawn, you can overseed, which means to scatter seeds over the existing lawn without special preparation. Overseeding should be done in early spring or in the fall. Spot seeding of bare places can be done at any time, but here again early spring or early fall is best. Keep the new grass moist until it is well established.

PLANTING A NEW LAWN

If you are moving in to a newly built house, you will either have to sod your lawn or plant it from scratch. And if your old lawn appears beyond repair, it may be easiest to start all over again. Replacing a lawn is harder than starting one from scratch, because the old lawn must be removed before the new one can be planted.

The old lawn must be dug up or chopped up before a new lawn can be planted. The old lawn can be dug up with a sod cutter. This machine slices off the top inch or so of soil, removing the whole thing, roots and all. The disadvantages of a sod cutter are disposing of the old sod and the fact that the newly exposed soil must be tilled.

The alternative is to use a power tiller. This turns the top few inches of the lawn into a mixture of well-prepared soil with plenty of organic matter.

In planting a new lawn, it is important to first make sure that the lawn has proper drainage. The ground should slope gently away from the house with no low spots and no steep slopes. The ground should be power-tilled to a depth of about 6 inches, particularly if heavy equipment used during construction packed down the soil around the house.

The soil should then be conditioned to ensure that it has the right acidity or alkalinity, and plenty of organic matter should be worked into the soil. It is easiest to work in the appropriate amount of lawn fertilizer at the same time that organic matter is being added. A sufficient amount of nitrogen should be added at this time, since the decaying organic matter will consume quite a bit of the nitrogen in the soil. Check with your local nursery for other specific soil problems in your area. Soil in the southwest, for example, tends to be low in iron, while eastern soils usually do better when potassium and phosphorus are added.

New grass is best planted at the start of its high growth season. In the north, grasses begin growth in the early spring. They generally also have a spurt of growth in the early fall. In warmer climates, the best-suited grasses usually grow at their fastest during the hot summer months. Grasses such as St. Augustine or Bermuda should be planted in the south in late spring or early summer. Try also to avoid planting new grass when weed growth is at a maximum. Perennial weeds parallel the growth of grasses, and nothing can be done about that. Annual weeds such as chickweed slow or stop their growth in the early fall. Crabgrass is usually killed by the first cold snap of fall. If your lawn is troubled by these types of weeds, time your planting accordingly.

You should not expect to see very much the first few weeks after planting a new lawn. Depending on the variety or varieties of grass planted, growth should be evident in the third to fourth week. Very fast growers, such as rye grass,

may even be ready for mowing by the fourth week. Lawns
planted with slow-growing varieties of grass may still look
thin after 6 to 8 weeks. Know the grass that you planted,
and don't overwater or overfeed if the lawn is not as dense
as you would like it.

COMMON TYPES OF GRASS

BENT: The major varieties include velvet bent, creeping
bent, and colonial bent. These grasses grow into a thick,
shiny green turf with a fine texture. They grow in cooler
regions and require a great deal of care. They tend to be
used more in professional applications, such as golf courses,
than for home lawns. Most bents are perennials. They prefer
a rich, moist, slightly acid soil with plenty of organic matter.
Bents do best in full sun, but can tolerate partial shade.
Newly sown grass should be kept moist until the plants are
well established, and fertilizer should be applied every other
month. Bents should be mowed regularly to keep the grass
less than an inch high. These grasses should be dethatched
in the early spring.

BERMUDA: Bermuda grass is a long-jointed grass that
spreads rapidly. There are various Bermuda hybrids, and
these grasses are well-known for producing beautiful lawns
with thickness and texture. They do not grow well, if at all,
in cooler climates. Bermuda grass grows best in rich, moist,
slightly acid soil. Most types require full sun. All varieties
are tolerant of salt air and salt spray. Bermuda grasses may
be grown from seed or from plugs set 6 to 9 inches apart.
They need to be fed at least 4 times a year, and as much as
6 times in the deep south. Mow regularly to keep the grass
about an inch high. Catching the clippings will reduce or
eliminate the need to dethatch in the spring.

BLUEGRASS: The main types are Kentucky bluegrass,
Canada bluegrass, and rough bluegrass. These are grown
in the northern part of the country for their rich green
color and dense growth. Canada and rough bluegrasses

tolerate cold climates and shady conditions. All are subject to fungus disease and to grub damage.

Kentucky bluegrass prefers full sun and rich, well-drained, slightly acid soil. It is drought resistant and will go dormant in very hot weather. It should be fertilized 3 times a year, early in each season: spring, summer, and fall. Mow regularly to a height of about 2 to 3 inches, letting it grow higher in hotter weather.

Canada bluegrass does well in dry soil and partial shade, preferring a slightly acid soil. Rough bluegrass grows in moist or even damp soil and cannot tolerate drought. Mow both to about 2½ inches high.

BUFFALO: Buffalo grass is native to the west and grows very slowly. It goes dormant in very hot weather and does best if not irrigated or overfed. It prefers a rich, well-drained soil, anywhere from slightly acid to slightly alkaline. It cannot tolerate shade or heavy rainfall. It should be fertilized twice a year, in early spring and early fall, and mowed to about 2 inches high.

CENTIPEDE: Centipede grass grows very slowly and rarely gets more than 5 inches tall. It is easy to maintain and is fairly drought resistant. It will tolerate a very acid soil and will grow in partial shade. It will not do well near the sea and requires regular watering. Fertilize in the spring and again in the early fall, and keep mowed to about 2 inches high.

FESCUE: The two major types are red fescue and tall fescue. This is a tough grass, used on athletic fields and for erosion control. Fescue is fairly drought resistant. It will grow in moist or dry slightly acid soil, and in full sun or partial shade. Fertilize in early spring and in late summer, and keep it mowed to about 2 inches high, 3 inches in hot weather.

RYE: There are two basic types of rye grass: annual and perennial. The annual grass is very fast to grow in the spring. In the south, it is often sown over a permanent lawn in the fall. It grows well through the winter and is then crowded out by the permanent grass in the spring.

Perennial rye only lives for about 5 years and can be used to grow a tough but temporary lawn even in cooler climates.

Rye grasses grow in soils ranging from acid to alkaline and can tolerate both partial shade and salt air. Rye grass should be fertilized if it has a yellowish tint and should be mowed regularly to about 2 inches high.

ST. AUGUSTINE: St. Augustine grass grows well in Florida and along the Gulf Coast, generally remaining green through the winter. It requires a very moist and slightly acid soil, and can tolerate salt air or spray. It is best planted from plugs in the spring. It should be fertilized 3 times a year and kept mowed to about 1½ inches high.

WHEAT GRASS: The two types are western wheat grass and crested wheat grass. They are very drought resistant and do not require irrigation. Both kinds go dormant during very hot weather. They do best in alkaline soil and require full sun. They should be fertilized in early spring and early fall, and should be mowed to a height of about 2 inches.

ZOYSIA: The major types of zoysia are Korean lawn grass, Manila grass, and Mascarene grass. They are salt tolerant and do best in warmer climates. They do best in slightly acid soil, but can tolerate a very wide range of conditions from acid to alkaline with proper water and feeding. These grasses will grow in conditions ranging from full sun to dense shade. They are best planted from plugs in early spring. They should be fertilized in early spring, summer, and early fall, and should be mowed to a 1½-inch height.

12

ORGANIC GARDENING

Organic gardening is gardening without the use of chemical fertilizers or poisonous insecticides. There are two primary reasons to garden organically. One is to keep chemicals and insecticides off of the food that you raise and eat. The other is to keep these substances out of the environment. Organic gardeners use natural minerals and nutrients instead of artificial, chemical plant foods. And organic gardeners do not use insecticides.

The foundation of organic gardening is soil preparation. As discussed earlier in this book, soil is a mixture of minerals, organic matter, water, and air. Depending on the various combination of these elements, the soil condition can be described as alkaline, neutral, or acid. Different plants grow best in different types of soil. Potatoes and raspberries, for example, do best in very acid soil. Peas or corn prefer a slightly acid soil. Beets and carrots do best in soil that is neutral to slightly alkaline. If the particular condition of the soil is not right for the plants that you want to grow, you must make changes to the soil. It is possible to make these changes by adding minerals to the soil. Excess acid in the soil, for example, can be neutralized by adding crushed limestone. An organic gardener changes the soil conditions by changing the mixture of minerals, organic matter, water, and air.

Plants can also be fertilized with organic nutrients, although it is harder to get a well-balanced, organic plant food this way than to buy it commercially. The problem is that sources of organic nutrients tend to have a relatively high concentration of one nutrient and are very much lacking in the others. For example, blood meal contains about 15% nitrogen, and very little potassium or phosphorus. Bone meal, on the other hand, is about 25% phosphorus and 3% nitrogen.

The primary organic source of plant nutrients is animal manure. Manure is relatively high in nitrogen, but does contain the other basic nutrients as well. Manure works best if it is composted before being used. Food-processing by-products, including bone meal, blood meal, and fish meal, are also good sources of nutrients. Food scraps and vegetable waste, such as peels, also provide nutrients, particularly when composted. There are also a number of important natural rock fertilizers. These include rock phosphate, which contains up to 50% phosphoric acid, and granite dust, which is high in potassium.

COMPOST

Organic gardening revolves around compost. Compost is the soil conditioner and fertilizer of the organic gardener. Compost is partially decomposed organic matter. When worked into the soil, it provides nutrients for plants. Compost also improves the composition of the soil, improving drainage and allowing plants to grow more easily and absorb nutrients more efficiently. Compost is made by layering different organic materials, which speeds up the decomposition. The basic ingredients of a compost heap are roughly equal volumes of carbon sources (leaves, straw, etc.) and nitrogen sources (grass clippings, manure, etc.). Some gardeners include a third ingredient consisting of soil and minerals such as limestone and phosphate rock.

The compost heap may just be a pile on the ground, but it is neater and more efficient if it is enclosed. This can be done by building a cage with chicken wire and wooden stakes, forming a cylinder out of snow fencing, or constructing a box out of old lumber, railroad ties, etc. The compost heap should be at least 4 feet across, and 3 to 4 feet high. Build up the compost heap with alternating layers of the various materials. Be sure to throw in any organic household garbage, such as potato peelings or uneaten leftovers. Dampen each layer with the garden hose as you add it to the heap.

The decomposing organic matter will generate temperatures up to 150 degrees at the center of the pile. Decomposition is quickest at the center, and the compost should be turned and stirred about once a week to ensure that everything decomposes evenly. The smaller the pieces of organic matter, the quicker they will decompose. If possible, chop up any large material before putting it in the compost heap. As the organic matter in the compost heap decomposes, the pile decreases in size. When it has reached about ½ its original volume, and the organic matter is broken up and has a dark rich color, use it in the garden. If you let the compost sit, it will continue to decompose, eventually disappearing without any benefit.

Compost should be worked into the soil before planting. It should be added annually, adding about 3 inches of compost to the soil.

MULCH

Mulch is anything that is used to cover the bare ground around a plant. You can mulch with dead leaves, bark, nut shells, grass clippings, or any other organic matter. Mulch protects plants against the cold in winter, it keeps the soil moist, it holds down weeds, and it eventually improves the soil structure and fertility as the organic matter decomposes.

Mulch also helps prevent damage to sprawling vegetables by keeping them off the ground.

There are three things to consider in choosing a mulch. The first is how the mulch will look in your garden. Pick a material that will blend in with your landscape. The second consideration is the effect of a particular mulch on your plants. And the third thing to consider is which materials are readily and cheaply available. If you live near a lumber mill, wood chips or sawdust may be available for the taking. If you don't, these materials may be expensive or unavailable.

Most people have grass clippings and leaves readily available, at little or no cost. Both are excellent for mulch. Grass clippings are rich in nitrogen and are very good for either composting or mulching. Leaves have all the basic plant nutrients and decompose rapidly. Leaves mat down well and seal in moisture, providing good protection against the cold. Other good organic mulch materials include grain hulls, nut shells, sawdust, wood chips, bark chips, stone, cornstalks, hay, straw, and pine needles.

INSECTICIDE ALTERNATIVES

Insects are a definite problem with some plants, and they must be removed to ensure the health of the plant and its produce. The simplest way to get rid of bugs in a small garden is to pick them off. This is time-consuming if not impossible if you have more than a few infected plants. Commercial insecticides may be dangerous both to the food that you harvest from the garden and, in the long term, to the environment. The alternatives are to use safe insecticides and to grow insect-resistant plants.

Dormant oil sprays are safe to plants and people and are effective against such chewing insects as aphids, mealybugs, and red spiders. The spray is used on dormant trees and shrubs in the spring before the buds open. You can buy an oil spray at your nursery. Spray directly on the plants. You cannot overapply dormant oil spray, as any excess just runs off.

Ryania is a plant-derived insecticide made from the ground-up roots of a South American plant. It is effective in controlling corn borers, coddling moths, and other insects.

Another plant-derived insecticide is rotenone. It can be safely used on all plants and has no effect on people or pets. It kills many types of insects, but is effective for only a short time.

Many plants growing in a garden tend to drive away insects. These include marigolds, asters, and chrysanthemums. Coriander and anise contain oils that can be used in an emulsion spray to kill spider mites and aphids.

Check with your local nursery to see which plants are insect resistant and to see what they can recommend as safe methods of reducing insect damage in your area.

13

❧━━━❦━━━❧

INDOOR FLOWERING PLANTS

Any plant can be grown indoors with some degree of success, but the most common houseplants are those that do not require a rest period during the winter. Some conditions indoors are not as good as outdoors for most plants. There is less light, temperatures are higher in the winter, humidity is different, and the plant has less room for its roots. On the other hand, the plant does not have to tolerate high winds, heavy rain or snow, or wide fluctuations in temperature. Indoor plants generally get a more consistent supply of food and water, and have less exposure to disease and pests (not counting house pets).

The best flowers for indoor growing are those that do best in the lower light levels and the combination of relatively high heat and low humidity found in most modern homes. House flowers also tend to be small, not requiring an extensive root system and not growing to be big and bushy. And a prime desirable characteristic of an indoor flowering plant is that it be in bloom almost constantly. Examples include African violets and wax begonias. Another choice is a plant that has attractive foliage when it is not in bloom, such as certain varieties of cactus. A third category is that of plants that do not bloom for a long period and are not really suited for indoor growing, but are so attractive that they are regularly grown in greenhouses and purchased for the home. These flowers, such as tulips, will bloom for a few weeks in the winter and be discarded.

The growing climate and environment not only varies from home to home, but there can be wide variations within a home. Higher floors tend to be warmer, and basements tend to be more humid. Bathrooms and kitchens are generally more humid than other rooms. Light varies depending on exposure. Matching the microclimates of your home with the requirements of plants will give you the best results.

When buying houseplants, look for a well-developed plant that is short and stocky, with abundant foliage. Developing buds are preferable to full blooms. Check leaves for rot or pest infestation. If buying houseplants in the winter, take care to protect them from the cold, even on a short drive home from the nursery.

All houseplants require light, but the amount needed varies from plant to plant. Some plants will need to be near a window on the south side of the house, while others will survive with much less light. In general, if the plant looks healthy, it is getting enough light. If it is tall and thin with sparse foliage, it is not getting enough light. It is difficult to give most houseplants too much light. But remember that houseplants, just like people, need a nightly rest in the dark.

Artificial light can be used to supplement or even replace natural daylight, although no artificial light is as beneficial as sunlight for growing. Any kind of electric light will aid in plant growth, but the best kind of light is that from fluorescent lamps specifically designed for growing. Again, remember that houseplants need some rest every night and don't expose them to more than about 14 hours of light a day.

Houseplants need regular watering, but it is likely that more plants are damaged by overwatering than by underwatering. Plant roots require both water and air. If they get too much water, they can't get enough air. And make sure that houseplants are not watered with cold water. The water should be at least room temperature, and warmer than that is even better. Watering is best done in the morning so the plant can make use of the water during the daylight hours.

Houseplants can adapt to a wide variety of chemicals in tap water, so in general if you can drink it, you can water your plants with it. The exception is highly chlorinated water. Use another source of water, or let the water stand for a day or two so that the chlorine evaporates before using it on plants. As a general rule, it is best to avoid getting water on plant leaves.

Houseplants can be watered in a variety of ways, and it is best to vary the watering method from time to time. One method is to water the plant from the top. This is best done with a watering can with a long spout so that you can avoid getting water on the leaves. Another way of watering houseplants is to put the pot in a saucer or bowl, fill the saucer with water, and let the plant draw up its own water. The water should be removed after about a half hour. The third method, one that is too laborious to do regularly, is to submerge the entire plant in a bucket of water. Make sure that the water level is above the soil level, and hold the plant in the water until there are no longer bubbles coming up from the plant. Let the plant drain well before returning it to its regular place.

Because of the low humidity in most homes, particularly in the winter, it may be necessary to increase the humidity for a particular houseplant. The easiest way is to move the plant to a more humid part of the house, such as the kitchen, the bathroom, or the basement. Plants can also be misted with a spray bottle of water. For very dry homes or particularly sensitive plants, cover the bottom of a tray with sand or fine gravel and add water, keeping it below the top of the fill material. Put the potted houseplants on the material, and the evaporating water will greatly increase the humidity around the plants.

Houseplants grow better if the temperature is cooler at night than during the day. Keep this in mind in picking out spots in the house for your plants. Also, houseplants should be kept away from cold winter drafts.

Garden soil is usually not well suited for potted plants. In addition to possible diseases and pests, the soil generally does not have enough organic matter to provide proper drainage and air circulation. Soil requirements vary from plant to plant, but most do well in a standard potting soil available from nurseries. This potting mixture is sterilized to remove pest eggs, diseases, and weeds. It is also premixed with the proper amount of organic matter and may contain nutrients. You may want to add some peat moss to open up the soil structure and some perlite to improve drainage.

It is important that the potting container have good drainage. Clay pots are porous. Moisture can escape through the walls, lessening the chance of damaging the plant by overwatering. Clay pots are heavy and can break. Plastic pots are lighter and generally have more drainage holes in the bottom to offset their nonporous material. The pot should be as small as possible without crowding the root system of the plant.

Larger pots should have some material in the bottom, below the soil, to aid drainage. In smaller pots, a piece or two of broken clay pot will do. In larger pots, put a layer of an inch or so of pebbles or gravel in the bottom before adding the soil. When repotting a houseplant, add enough potting soil to the new pot so that the root ball of the plant sits just below the rim of the pot. Place the plant in the new pot and add potting soil until the soil level is just at the top of the root ball. Tap the pot on a hard surface occasionally as you add soil to tamp it down and eliminate air pockets. For the first watering, water the plant completely, and then do not water it again until the soil looks dry and crumbly. Repotting should be done when the houseplant becomes pot bound. This happens when the roots of the plant completely fill the soil and the pot. The plant may wilt, or you may see the roots struggling out of the drain holes in the bottom of the pot. If you suspect that a plant is pot bound, make sure that the soil is damp enough to hold together, and remove the plant from its pot. Hold your hand over the top of the pot, turn it upside down, and rap it on the edge of a table. The root ball will come out in your hand. If it is pot bound, the roots will be thick and tangled and matted.

Houseplants need to be fed regularly, but the organic fertilizers used outdoors are not well suited to indoor use. Organic fertilizers work too slowly for most houseplants, and may have too strong an odor for indoor use. Chemical fertilizers designed for houseplants all work well with most plants. They come in several forms, including powders, liquids, and tablets. All work well if directions are followed.

Many houseplants do better if they are put outside for a time in spring or summer. The response varies from plant to plant, and some, such as African violets, are better left inside. Houseplants put outside should be sheltered from strong winds or driving rain, and may require a gradual shift to full sunlight.

New plants can be grown from seed, but only by vegetative reproduction from the original plant can you be sure that the new plant will be just like the one you already have. Vegetative reproduction means growing a new plant from a part of the old one.

The simplest and easiest form of vegetative reproduction is propagation through stem cuttings. Take a cutting of the plant's stem during active growth, cutting from the current year's growth. Avoid cutting a stem that has flowers or buds. The cutting will usually be 3 to 6 inches long, varying from plant to plant. The cutting should contain 2 to 6 nodes (leaf joints), making the cut just below the lower node.

Dip the end of the stem cutting in rooting hormone, available from your local nursery. Make a small hole in a pot filled with potting soil. Hold the cutting upright in the hole while filling it up with coarse sand. Cover the pot with clear plastic, propped up so that it doesn't touch the plant. This will hold in moisture and raise the humidity around the plant. Once the stem cutting becomes established and there is some new growth, loosen the plastic for a few days and then remove it.

Some plants, such as African violets, send up multiple clumps of stems from the soil. These clumps are joined below the soil, but they can be separated and replanted as new houseplants.

POPULAR FLOWERING HOUSEPLANTS

ACALYPHA: This plant produces large plumes of fuzzy red flowers that grow as long as 20 inches. It has dark green leaves and will bloom year round under the right conditions. Acalyphas do best in direct sunlight and prefer a small temperature variation from day to night. Their soil should be kept moist, and they should be fed monthly. Prune older plants in the spring, leaving about a foot of growth. Acalypha can be propagated from stem cuttings in the summer.

ACHIMENES: Also called magic flower or widow's tear. This plant produces a large mass of satiny flowers about 2 inches across. Achimenes grow up to a foot high, with blooms in a wide variety of colors, including blue, pink, yellow, and red. They grow well and look good in hanging containers. They prefer indirect sunlight and do well under artificial light. They should be planted in a mixture of potting soil, sand, and peat moss, and kept moist, particularly while blooming. Achimenes become dormant after blooming and should be stored in plastic bags over the winter.

AECHMEA: Aechmea produces a central spike blossom up to 2 feet high, with broad leaves up to 10 inches long. They do best in bright but indirect sunlight and should be potted in an equal mixture of sand and peat moss. Keep the mixture moist, and fertilize the plant monthly. The leaves form a cup at the base of the plant. This should be kept filled with water. Small shoots will appear at the base of the plant after flowering. These can be replanted to grow new plants.

AESCHYNANTHUS: Also known as basketvines, these plants send out long trailing stems tipped with 2-to-4-inch flowers. They require at least 4 hours of direct sunlight a day, particularly during the winter. They should be planted in a mixture of 1 part sand, 1 part potting soil, and 2 parts peat moss. This mixture should be kept moist, and the plant should be fertilized monthly.

AFRICAN VIOLET: The actual name is saintpaulia. There are thousands of varieties of this plant. They produce clusters of small flowers and bloom continuously with proper care. The plants usually grow to about 6 inches high. They grow well in bright sunlight, in filtered light, or under 14 to 16 hours of artificial light per day. They should be planted in a mixture of 1 part potting soil, 1 part sand, and 2 parts peat moss. They should be watered regularly and fed monthly.

AGAPANTHUS: These plants are also called lily of the Nile or blue African lily. They have long leaves and clusters of lilylike flowers on tall stems that grow up to 2 feet high. Agapanthus does best with about 4 hours of direct sunlight a day, but should be shaded from more than that in the summer. They prefer fairly cool nights. Keep the soil moist, and feed every other week during the growing season. Do not feed the rest of the year.

ALLAMANDA: Viny plants that grow up to 4 feet high, producing 4-to-5-inch-wide yellow flowers in the spring and summer. They require at least 4 hours of direct sunlight per day. Keep the soil moist and feed every two weeks during the growing season. Do not feed the rest of the year. Allamanda can be propagated from stem cuttings in the spring.

AMAZON LILY: See EUCHARIS

ANGRAECUM: This is a miniature orchid, growing only to about 5 inches high. It produces dozens of tiny white blossoms on spreading stems. Angraecum does best in bright indirect sunlight and prefers cooler nights. It should be planted in a potting medium of 2 parts fir bark and 1 part peat moss. It should be kept moist and does best in a humid environment.

APHELANDRA: These plants have broad dark leaves and bright flower clusters up to 6 to 8 inches high. They are generally pruned to about 18 inches high. They should be planted in a mixture of 1 part sand, 1 part potting soil, and 2 parts peat moss. Keep the planting mixture moist, particularly during the spring and summer. Fertilize every other week during the blooming season. Aphelandra can be propagated from stem cuttings during the spring.

APOSTLE PLANT: See **NEOMARICA**

ARDISIA: This plant produces large clusters of small red berries during the winter, making it a favorite Christmas decoration. They can grow up to 3 feet high, appearing tree-like after they lose their lower leaves. Ardisias prefer bright but indirect sunlight and cooler nights. The soil should be kept moist, and they should be fed every other week. They can be propagated in the spring from stem cuttings.

AZALEA: Azaleas produce large clusters of 2-to-4-inch blossoms in late winter or early spring. The plants grow up to 2 feet tall. They require at least 4 hours of direct sunlight daily and prefer very cool night temperatures. They should be planted in a mixture of 1 part sand, 1 part potting soil, and 2 parts peat moss. Keep the potting mixture moist, and feed every other week from the time the flowers fade until new buds appear. Do not feed while the plants are flowering. Azaleas can be propagated from stem cuttings.

AZTEC LILY: See **STAPELIA**

BASKETVINE: See **AESCHYNANTHUS**

BEEFSTEAK PLANT: See **ACALYPHA**

BEGONIA: The most popular species, the wax begonia, has small satiny flowers with oval leaves up to 4 inches across. They bloom continuously, growing up to a foot high. Begonias require at least 4 hours of direct sunlight a day and prefer very cool nights. They should be planted in a mixture of potting soil and peat moss. Wax begonias should be allowed to dry slightly between waterings during the growing season. Other varieties should be kept moist. Begonias should be fed every other week during the growing season. All varieties can be propagated from stem cuttings.

BELLFLOWER: Bellflowers produce a large number of small (1-to-1½-inch) flowers, blooming in the summer and early fall. The colors vary with species, generally running to white, blue, and purple. They have trailing stems that show well in hanging baskets. Bellflowers require at least 4 hours of direct sunlight a day and prefer cooler nights. They should be planted in a mixture of 1 part sand, 1 part potting soil, and 2 parts peat moss. The mixture should be kept moist and fertilized monthly during the growing season. Do not feed the rest of the year, and cut back on the watering.

BIRD-OF-PARADISE FLOWER: See **STRELITZIA**

BLACK-EYED-SUSAN VINE: See **THUNBERGIA**

BLOOD LILY: See **HAEMANTHUS**

BLUE AFRICAN LILY: See **AGAPANTHUS**

BLUE SAGE: See **ERANTHEMUM**

BOUGAINVILLEA: These are tropical vines that grow fast and produce bright clusters of small flowers. They will bloom almost continuously with proper care and conditions. They require at least 4 hours of direct sunlight each day and don't require particularly cool nights. The soil should be allowed to dry between waterings, and they should be fed every other week during the growing season. Do not feed during the rest of the year. Bougainvillea can be propagated from stem cuttings in the spring.

BROWALLIA: Browallias have thin, trailing stems that grow up to 3 feet long. They produce clusters of 1-to-2-inch flowers, usually blue or white, all year. They require at least 4 hours of direct sunlight throughout the winter, but should have indirect light the rest of the year. They prefer cooler nights. Browallias should be planted in a mixture of 1 part sand, 1 part potting soil, and 2 parts peat moss. Keep the planting mixture moist, and feed the plants monthly during the winter, every other week the rest of the year. They can be propagated from stem cuttings in the summer.

BRUNFELSIA: Also known as the chameleon plant; the flowers change color from purple to lavender to white within the first few days of blooming. They can bloom all year with proper care and conditions, but generally rest for a few weeks in spring. They require at least 4 hours of direct sunlight during the winter and prefer indirect light the rest of the year. They do best with fairly cool nights. The soil should be kept moist, and the plants should be fertilized every other week during the growing season. Do not feed the rest of the year, and cut back on the watering.

CALCEOLARIA: Calceolaria is also known as slipper-wort and as pocketbook flower. It has large leaves and saclike blossoms about 2 inches across. It blooms in a variety of colors in the spring. It can grow up to 2 feet high. Calceolaria does best in indirect or filtered sunlight and prefers very cool nights. The soil should be watered just enough to keep it moist during the day and care should be taken to avoid getting the foliage wet. Do not feed during the growing season. It can be propagated from stem cuttings in the fall.

CALLA LILY: See **ZANTEDESCHIA**

CALLIANDRA: Also known as powder puffs, these plants produce 2-to-3-inch fluffy blossoms, blooming during the winter and spring. They can grow to be very bushy and are usually trimmed to about 3 feet high. They require at least 4 hours of direct sunlight each day and don't need particularly cool nights. The soil should be kept just damp, and they should be fertilized monthly through the spring and summer. Calliandras should be pruned in late spring or early summer and can be propagated from stem cuttings in the spring.

CAMELLIA: These plants produce large (5-inch) flowers in white, pink, or red. They usually only bloom for about 6 weeks, in late fall to early spring, depending on the species. They can grow to be somewhat tall and are usually trimmed to about 3 feet or less. They prefer bright but indirect sunlight and very cool nights. Camellias should be planted in a mixture of 1 part sand, 1 part potting soil, and 2 parts peat moss. Keep the mixture moist, and feed with a fertilizer specifically made for camellias in early spring, late spring, and early summer. They can be propagated from stem cuttings in early summer.

CAPE COWSLIP: See **LACHENALIA**

CAPE PRIMROSE: See **STREPTOCARPUS**

CAPSICUM: Capsicum produces tiny white flowers and colorful 2-to-3-inch chile peppers. They grow up to a foot high and bear fruit after about 6 months. They require at least 4 hours of direct sunlight a day and don't need very cool nights. Capsicums should be kept moist and should not be fertilized. They can be propagated from seed in early spring.

CATTLEYA: A common orchid often used in corsages, cattleyas produce 6-inch flowers on top of 12-to-18 inch stalks. They require at least 4 hours of direct sunlight per day, but should be shaded from very hot sun during the summer. They should be potted in a mixture of 2 parts fir bark and 1 part peat moss. Like all orchids, they prefer a humid environment. They should be fed monthly with a high-nitrogen fertilizer.

CESTRUM: Cestrum includes day-blooming jasmine, night-blooming jasmine, and willow-leaved jasmine. The plants are very fragrant, and their small flowers bloom throughout the year. The blossoms are followed by small black berries. Cestrum plants grow tall and thin, and are generally pinched off to keep them about 2 feet high. They require at least 4 hours of direct sunlight a day and don't need very cool nights. Keep the soil moist and feed the plants every few months. They can be propagated by stem cuttings at any time.

CHAMELEON PLANT: See **BRUNFELSIA**

CHRYSANTHEMUM: Chrysanthemums, which include the marguerite, produce large numbers of 3-inch flowers in white, pink, or yellow that bloom throughout the year. They require at least 4 hours of direct sunlight daily and prefer fairly cool nights. The soil should be kept moist, and the plants should be fed every other week. They can be propagated by stem cuttings in the early spring.

CLIVIA: These plants are also called Kafir lilies. They are bulb plants that bloom in the winter, producing clusters of bright 3-inch flowers on foot-high stalks. They do best in indirect sunlight, with cool nights. The soil should be allowed to dry out between waterings from winter to late summer, with monthly feedings during this period. In the fall, they should not be fed and should receive minimal water. They can be propagated in the spring by bulb division.

COLUMNEA: Columneas grow with stems that reach up to 4 feet long, producing 2-to-4 inch tubular flowers. They do well in hanging containers. They grow best in indirect sunlight and can also be grown under 14 to 16 hours of artificial light per day. They do not need cool nights. Columneas should be planted in a mixture of 1 part sand, 1 part potting soil, and 2 parts peat moss. The mixture should be kept moist, and the plants should be fed monthly. They can be propagated by stem cuttings in the summer.

CORAL PLANT: See **RUSSELIA**

CROCUS: There are many varieties of crocus, and most make good winter houseplants. They grow 4 to 5 inches high and produce 2-inch blossoms. Crocuses require at least

4 hours of direct sunlight a day and prefer fairly cool nights. The soil should be kept moist while the foliage is green, and they should not be fertilized. Florists and nurseries sell fully blossoming plants during the winter.

CROSSANDRA: Crossandras have salmon-orange flowers that bloom year round. The flowers appear about 9 months after planting, and the plants grow to about a foot high. Crossandras require at least 4 hours of direct sunlight a day except during the hottest part of summer, when they should be partially shaded. They do best in fairly constant temperatures from day to night. Plant in a mixture of 1 part sand, 1 part potting soil, and 2 parts peat moss. Keep the soil moist and fertilize every other week. Crossandras can be planted from seed or propagated from stem cuttings at any time.

CYCLAMEN: Cyclamens produce delicate pink, red, or white flowers 2 to 3 inches long. They have thick green leaves with silver markings. The plants grow to about a foot high and bloom from midautumn to spring. They prefer indirect sunlight and cool nights. Cyclamens should be planted in a mixture of 1 part sand, 1 part potting soil, and 2 parts peat moss. Keep the soil moist and fertilize every other week. They can be planted from seed in the spring. Take care to repot as needed.

DAFFODIL: See NARCISSUS

DAPHNE: Daphne produces clusters of small pink-to-red flowers with a sweet fragrance. The flowers bloom from late fall to early spring. Daphnes are best pruned to keep them under 2 feet high. They do best in indirect sunlight and cooler nights. They should be watered lightly and fed once a year in the spring. Daphnes can be propagated in the summer from stem cuttings.

DIPLADENIA: These are viny plants that produce silky 3-inch flowers resembling morning glories. They should be pruned by pinching back the tips of the stems to keep the plant under 3 feet high. They do best in indirect sunlight and fairly constant temperatures. Allow the soil to dry out between waterings. Fertilize every other week. Dipladenia can be propagated in the spring by stem cuttings.

EASTER LILY: These plants produce 6-to-8-inch white, fragrant flowers that bloom for about a week. The plants grow up to 3 feet high. They do best in indirect sunlight when in bloom, and prefer cool nights. Keep the soil moist when in bloom, and do not feed. Easter lilies are difficult to grow at home and are just as well purchased from a florist. They do much better outdoors in warm weather.

EPIPHYLLUM: Also called orchid cactus, this plant has neither leaves nor spines. The bright, fragrant flowers grow directly from the stems, growing from 2 to 10 inches across depending on the variety. They do best in indirect sunlight and prefer cool nights. They should be planted in a mixture of 1 part sand, 1 part potting soil, and 2 parts peat moss. Keep the soil moist and fertilize every other week during spring and summer. The rest of the year, keep the soil fairly dry and do not feed. Epiphyllum can be propagated from stem cuttings in the summer.

ERANTHEMUM: Also called blue sage, this plant produces spikes of blue flowers in the winter and spring. They grow up to 2 feet high. Eranthemums require at least 4 hours of direct sunlight a day during the winter and prefer light shade in the summer. Keep the soil moist and feed every other week during the growing season. Do not feed in spring and summer. Prune the plant back to about 5 inches high at the end of summer. They can be propagated from stem cuttings.

EUCHARIS: Also known as Amazon lily, these plants grow up to 2 feet high and produce clusters of 2-inch white flowers. They bloom 2 to 3 times a year. They do best in indirect sunlight and constant temperatures. Plant in a mixture of 1 part sand, 1 part potting soil, and 2 parts peat moss. Keep the soil very moist during the growing season.

FOUNTAIN PLANT: See RUSSELIA

FUCHSIA: Fuchsias have 2-to-3-inch flowers on tall stems, growing up to 3 feet tall. Many blossom throughout the year. They require at least 4 hours of direct sunlight a day, except during the summer, when they should be shaded from the hottest sun. They prefer cool nights. When the plant is flowering, keep the soil moist and fertilize every other week. The rest of the year, feed once a month and keep the soil a little drier. Summer flowering plants should be pruned to about 6 inches high during their dormant period. Propagate from stem cuttings.

GARDENIA: The most commonly grown gardenias produce 3-inch white flowers on bushes 2 to 3 feet high. They blossom in winter and spring. Larger varieties can also be grown indoors. Gardenias require at least 4 hours of direct sunlight a day. They will not grow new buds if night temperatures are above 65 degrees. They should be planted in a mixture of 1 part sand, 1 part potting soil, and 2 parts peat moss. Keep the soil moist and fertilize once a month. Gardenias can be propagated from stem cuttings.

GERANIUM: There are many types of geraniums well suited for indoor growing. The most common, the zonal geranium, grows up to 3 feet high and produces red, white, or pink flowers up to 4 inches across. They do best with at least 4 hours of direct sunlight a day and prefer cool nights. Allow the soil to dry between waterings. Fertilize every other week from spring through fall, and once a month during the winter. Geraniums can be propagated from stem cuttings at any time.

GLORIOSA: These viny plants grow up to 4 feet high, producing 3-to-4-inch flowers resembling lilies (they are sometimes called climbing lilies). They alternate stages of flowering and dormancy. They can be planted at any time, but the normal blooming season is late summer to early fall. Gloriosas require at least 4 hours of direct sunlight a day and prefer fairly constant temperatures. While they

are flowering, keep the soil moist and fertilize every other week.

GLOXINERA: These are hybrids with a wide variety of
colors and shapes. Taller varieties grow up to 6 inches high
with 1-inch flowers. They do best in indirect sunlight, and
can be grown in 14 to 16 hours of artificial light daily.
They prefer fairly constant temperatures. They should be
planted in a mixture of 1 part sand, 1 part potting soil, and
2 parts peat moss. Keep the soil moist and fertilize once
a month during the growing season. After blossoming, do
not feed and keep fairly dry. They can be propagated from
stem cuttings at any time.

GLOXINIA: See **SINNINGIA**

GRAPE HYACINTH: See **MUSCARI**

HAEMANTHUS: Also called blood lilies because of the
color of their flowers. They produce 6-to-12-inch flower
clusters made up of small tubular blossoms at the top of a
tall stem up to 18 inches high. They require at least 4 hours
of direct sunlight a day and prefer cooler nights. Keep the
soil moist and fertilize once a month during the growing
season. During late fall and winter, keep fairly dry and do
not feed.

HELIOTROPE: This is a very fragrant flower, with hybrids
producing blooms in lavender, blue, purple, and white. They
can be grown as bushy plants up to a foot high, or trained
and pruned as a single long stem, up to 4 feet long. Heliotropes require at least 4 hours of direct sunlight a day and
prefer cooler nights. Keep the soil moist and fertilize every
other week. They can be propagated from stem cuttings at
any time.

HIBISCUS: These plants bloom year round, with flowers
up to 5 inches across. They should be kept under 3 feet
high by pruning, and they can live up to 20 to 25 years.
Hibiscuses require at least 4 hours of direct sunlight a day
and prefer fairly constant temperatures. Keep the soil moist

and fertilize once a month. They can be propagated from stem cuttings.

HOYA: Also known as wax plants, hoyas are vines with 3-inch leaves and 1-inch fragrant, waxy-looking flowers. They do best with about 4 hours of direct sunlight a day, but can be grown in indirect light. They prefer fairly constant temperatures. Allow the soil to dry between waterings when the plants are not in bloom. Fertilize every other month in spring and summer. It is best to train the vines to grow on a small trellis. They may be propagated by stem cuttings at any time.

HYACINTH: Hyacinths produce sweet-smelling, waxy-looking flowers in large clumps in a wide variety of colors. They require partial shade while flowering, but at other times do best with direct sunlight for at least 4 hours a day. Keep the soil moist while the plants are flowering, allowing some drying at other times. Hyacinths prefer very cool temperatures at night.

HYDRANGEA: Hydrangeas produce large clusters of white, red, pink, purple, lavender, or blue flowers. The 1-inch flowers grow in 8-to-10-inch clusters, and the plants grow about 2 feet tall. They do best in indirect sunlight and prefer cooler night temperatures. Keep the soil very moist and do not fertilize. Hydrangeas are very difficult to maintain from one year to another.

IMPATIENS: Also called patient Lucy, these plants are easy to grow and bloom year round. They grow up to a foot high and produce soft flowers 1 to 2 inches across in a wide variety of colors. Impatiens do best in indirect sunlight or in 14 to 16 hours of artificial light a day. They should be planted in a mixture of 1 part sand, 1 part potting soil, and 2 parts peat moss. Keep the soil moist and fertilize every other week. They can be propagated at any time from stem cuttings or from seeds.

IPOMOEA: More commonly called morning glories, these are usually thought of as summer garden plants but can be grown easily indoors during the winter. They are viny plants, producing flowers 4 to 8 inches across in blue, purple, red, pink, or white. Morning glories require at least 4 hours of direct sunlight a day and prefer fairly constant temperatures. Keep the soil barely moist and fertilize monthly.

JASMINE: Jasmine has a sweet fragrance and produces clusters of small flowers in a wide variety of colors. Jasmine requires at least 4 hours of direct sunlight a day and prefers very cool nights. Keep the soil moist and fertilize every other week except when the plants are dormant. Prune regularly to keep the plants under 3 feet high.

JERUSALEM CHERRY: See **SOLANUM**

KAFIR LILY: See **CLIVIA**

KALANCHOE: These plants bloom for many weeks in the winter, growing about a foot high and producing large clusters of small red or yellow flowers. Kalanchoes require at least 4 hours of direct sunlight a day and prefer cool nights. Allow the soil to dry between waterings, and fertilize every other week.

KOHLERIA: Kohlerias grow up to 2 feet high, producing five-petal flowers in a wide variety of colors. They grow best in indirect sunlight or under 14 to 16 hours a day of artificial light. They prefer fairly constant temperatures. Keep the soil moist and fertilize once a month while the plants are growing. Cut back the plants during the dormant period. Kohlerias can be propagated from stem cuttings.

LACHENALIA: Also called Cape cowslips, these are bulb plants that grow easily and reach up to a foot high. They often have purple spotted leaves and produce yellow, red, and purple flowers. They do best with at least 4 hours of direct sunlight a day and prefer very cool nights. Keep the soil moist and fertilize once a month during the growing season.

LAELIA: This is an orchid that produces clusters of yellow 2-inch blossoms on spikes about 18 inches tall. They generally require at least 4 hours of direct sunlight a day, but should be shaded from the hottest sun during the summer. Plant in a mixture of 2 parts fir bark and 1 part peat moss. Allow the mixture to partially dry between waterings, and fertilize once a month.

LILY OF THE NILE: See **AGAPANTHUS**

LILY-OF-THE-VALLEY ORCHID: These plants produce foot-high spikes of small waxy-looking white flowers that last 6 to 8 weeks and have a strong fragrance. They require at least 4 hours of direct sunlight a day, but should be shaded from very strong midday sun. They prefer slightly cool nights. They should be planted in a mixture of 2 parts fir bark and 1 part peat moss, which should be allowed to dry between waterings.

LOBULARIA: Also called sweet alyssum, these small plants grow 5 to 10 inches high and produce clusters of tiny, fragrant flowers. Most varieties are grown as annuals and discarded after flowering. They require at least 4 hours of direct sunlight a day and prefer cool nights. Keep the soil moist and fertilize once a month. The single-flower type should be propagated from seed in the late summer. The double-flower variety can be propagated from stem cuttings at any time.

MAGIC FLOWER: See **ACHIMENES**

MALVAVISCUS: Also called Turk's cap or Scotch purse, this is a bushy plant growing to about 2 feet high. It produces 2-inch red flowers that bloom year round, but never fully open. They require at least 4 hours of direct sunlight a day and prefer fairly constant temperatures. Keep the soil moist and fertilize every other week. They can be propagated from stem cuttings at any time.

MARGUERITE: See **CHRYSANTHEMUM**

MAXILLARIA: This is an easily grown orchid whose fragrant blooms last for a long time. The plants grow to about a foot high, and the flowers are 1 to 2 inches long and are red with yellow speckles. They do best in indirect sunlight and prefer cool nights. They should be planted in a mixture of 2 parts fir bark and 1 part peat moss. Keep the mixture moist at all times and fertilize once a month.

MEXICAN FLAME VINE: See **SENECIO**

MORNING GLORY: See **IPOMOEA**

MUSCARI: Also called grape hyacinth, these plants produce 6-to-8-inch spikes of tiny deep blue flowers in mid-winter to early spring. The plants grow up to a foot high and have grasslike leaves. Grape hyacinths do best with at least 4 hours of direct sunlight a day and prefer fairly cool nights. Keep the soil moist until the foliage withers, and do not fertilize.

NARCISSUS: There are two kinds of narcissus that are generally grown as houseplants. The large trumpet-flowered type are also called daffodils, and have 4-inch flowers and 10-to-12-inch leaves. The other type, more generally called narcissus, have 4 to 8 smaller flowers on each stem. Narcissi grow best in indirect sunlight and prefer fairly cool nights. They are very difficult to propagate at home.

NASTURTIUM: See **TROPAEOLUM**

NEOMARICA: Also called the Apostle plant or twelve apostles, neomarica resembles iris, growing 12 to 18 inches high and producing fragrant flowers with white outer petals and blue inner petals. The flowers only last a day, but the plants bloom for a long period in winter. Neomarica does best in indirect sunlight and prefers cool nights. Keep the soil moist and fertilize once a month.

NICOTIANA: These are dwarf varieties of flowering tobacco. The plants grow to about 10 inches high and produce trumpet-shaped flowers 2 inches across in a wide variety of colors. Nicotianas require at least 4 hours a day of direct sunlight and prefer slightly cool nights. Keep the soil moist and fertilize every other week. They are grown as annuals and discarded after flowering.

ORCHID CACTUS: See **EPIPHYLLUM**

OSMANTHUS: Also called sweet olive, these plants produce clusters of tiny white flowers with orange-blossom fragrance. They bloom throughout the year. They do best in direct sunlight and prefer cool nights. Keep the soil moist and fertilize once a month. They can be propagated from stem cuttings in the summer.

OXALIS: These are very small plants, growing only 4 to 6 inches high, and producing satiny 1-inch flowers from fall through spring. The blossoms open only on sunny days, closing at night and on cloudy days. Oxalis requires at least 4 hours of direct sunlight a day and prefers cooler nights. Keep the soil moist and fertilize once a month during the growing season.

PARLOR IVY: See **SENECIO**

PASSIONFLOWER: This is a viny plant that produces very unusual large flowers, with large outer petals surrounding an intricate inner crown. Passionflowers do best with at least 4 hours of direct sunlight a day and prefer cool nights. Keep the soil moist and fertilize every other week during the growing season. They can be propagated from stem cuttings at any time.

PATIENT LUCY: See **IMPATIENS**

PETUNIA: Petunias last a single winter growing season indoors, producing flowers up to 4 inches across in a wide variety of colors. The plants can grow up to a foot high.

They do best with at least 4 hours of direct sunlight a day. They require cool night temperatures during the winter or they will not bloom. Allow the soil to dry between waterings and fertilize every other week.

POCKETBOOK FLOWER: See **CALCEOLARIA**

POWDER PUFF: See **CALLIANDRA**

PRIMROSE: The most common variety, fairy primrose, produces clusters of red, pink, or white flowers on 8-to-10-inch stalks. These plants are usually bought in flower from florists and discarded after blossoming. They can, however, be planted in the garden as perennials. Primroses do best in indirect sunlight and prefer cool nights. Keep the soil moist and fertilize every other week. They are difficult to propagate at home.

RECHSTEINERIA: These are long-blooming houseplants with 1-to-2-inch tubular flowers and heart-shaped leaves. One variety, the cardinal flower, blooms most of the year if old stems are removed. They do best in indirect sunlight, but can tolerate direct sunlight in winter. They prefer fairly constant temperatures and should be planted in a mixture of 1 part sand, 1 part potting soil, and 2 parts peat moss. Allow the soil to dry between waterings, and avoid getting any water on the leaves. Fertilize once a month during the growing season. They can be propagated from stem cuttings in late winter or early spring.

ROSA: Miniature roses will bloom year round indoors. They produce small fragrant flowers in red, yellow, and pink, and the plants grow to about a foot high. Miniature roses require at least 4 hours of direct sunlight a day and prefer cool nights. Keep the soil moist and fertilize every other week. They can be propagated from stem cuttings at any time.

ROSEMARY: Useful for cooking, rosemary also produces small fragrant blue flowers that bloom from midwinter to early spring. They are generally pruned to under 15 inches by pinching off the stem tips, which are used for seasoning. They can be propagated from stem cuttings when the tips are firm.

RUELLIA: Also known as the trailing velvet plant, this is a 2-to-3-foot-high plant that produces pink bell-shaped flowers in winter. They do best in indirect light and slightly cool nights. They should be planted in a mixture of 1 part sand, 1 part potting soil, and 2 parts peat moss. Keep the soil moist and fertilize every other week during the planting season. Water less often and do not feed while the plant is dormant.

RUSSELIA: Also known as the coral plant or the fountain plant, russelias produce 1-to-2-inch tubular flowers on arching branches up to 3 feet across. They are usually planted in hanging baskets. Russelias prefer at least 4 hours of direct sunlight a day and cool nights. Allow the soil to dry between waterings, and fertilize every other week. They can be propagated from stem cuttings in the summer.

SAINTPAULIA: See **AFRICAN VIOLET**

SAXIFRAGA: These are also known as strawberry geranium and strawberry begonia. They are small dense plants with reddish-green leaves and long wiry stalks that produce tiny white flowers in summer. They do best in partial shade and prefer very cool nights. Allow the soil to dry between waterings, and fertilize every 3 months.

SCARBOROUGH LILY: See **VALLOTA**

SCILLA: These plants bloom in midwinter indoors, producing waxy-looking bell-shaped flowers and long green leaves. They grow up to a foot high, with 6-inch spikes of flowers. Scillas grow well in full sun to partial shade and prefer very cool nights. Bulbs should be potted in early fall and left in a cool dark place for 8 to 10 weeks before being brought into the light. Keep the soil moist during the growing season and do not fertilize.

SCOTCH PURSE: See **MALVAVISCUS**

SENECIO: Varieties include the Mexican flame vine and parlor ivy. They produce brightly colored flowers and may bloom throughout the year. They do best with at least 4 hours of direct sunlight a day during the winter and partial shade the rest of the year. Keep the soil moist and fertilize once a month. Cut the plants back after flowering to encourage growth.

SINNINGIA: These plants are more commonly referred to as gloxinias. They produce velvety bell-shaped flowers 3 to 6 inches across, in red, white, pink, lavender, or purple. The plants go through alternating periods of flowering and dormancy. Gloxinias do best in indirect sunlight or can be grown under 14 to 16 hours of artificial light a day. They prefer constant temperatures and should be planted in a mixture of 1 part sand, 1 part potting soil, and 2 parts peat moss. Keep the soil moist, and fertilize once a month during the growing season.

SLIPPERWORT: See **CALCEOLARIA**

SOLANUM: Also known as Jerusalem cherry, this plant grow up to a foot high. It produces small white flowers in late summer and early fall, followed by cherry-sized fruit in midwinter. The fruit is not edible. Jerusalem cherry requires at least 4 hours of direct sunlight a day and prefers fairly cool nights. Allow the soil to dry between waterings, and fertilize once a month.

STAPELIA: Also known as Aztec lilies, these plants produce a single orchidlike flower on top of a foot-high stalk. The flowers are red and about 4 inches across. Aztec lilies require at least 4 hours of direct sunlight a day and prefer fairly constant temperatures during the growing season. Keep the soil moist and fertilize once a month while the foliage is green. Do not feed while the plant is dormant.

STAR JASMINE: These plants produce small, starlike flowers on slow-growing vines. They can be grown on trellises or pinched back and grown as small bushes. They do best with at least 4 hours of direct sunlight a day in winter and indirect sunlight the rest of the year. They prefer cool nights. Allow the soil to dry between waterings, and fertilize every few months. They can be propagated from stem cuttings in fall or winter.

STEPHANOTIS: These viny plants produce very fragrant white flowers from late spring through fall. The 1-inch waxy-looking flowers grow in 6-inch clusters. The plant can be grown as vines with support or as a small bushy plant by pinching back the tips of new stems. It does best with at least 4 hours of direct sunlight a day and prefers fairly constant temperatures. Keep the soil moist, and fertilize once a month from early spring to early fall. Do not feed during the winter.

STRAWBERRY BEGONIA: See **SAXIFRAGA**

STRAWBERRY GERANIUM: See **SAXIFRAGA**

STRELITZIA: Also known as the bird-of-paradise flower, this plant produces flowers resembling the heads of tropical birds. The plants grow 2 to 3 feet high, and they bloom in late summer and early fall. They prefer at least 4 hours of direct sunlight a day and cool nights. Allow the soil to dry between waterings, and fertilize every other week. They should be grown in large containers and divided only when necessary.

STREPTOCARPUS: Also known as Cape primrose, these plants produce 3-to-5-inch-wide trumpet-shaped flowers in white, red, pink, blue, or purple. They do best in indirect sunlight and can be grown under 14 to 16 hours of artificial light a day. They prefer constant temperatures. They should be planted in a mixture of 1 part sand, 1 part potting soil, and 2 parts peat moss. Keep the soil moist and fertilize once a month during the growing season.

STREPTOSOLEN: These plants produce large clusters of bright orange flowers and do well in hanging containers. They require at least 4 hours of direct sunlight a day in winter and prefer partial shade in summer. Keep the soil moist and fertilize once a month. They can be propagated from stem cuttings at any time.

SWEET ALYSSUM: See **LOBULARIA**

SWEET OLIVE: See **OSMANTHUS**

THUNBERGIA: Also known as the black-eyed Susan vine, this plant produces 1-to-2-inch flowers with black centers and white, yellow, or orange petals. The viny stems grow up to 4 feet long and can be grown on a trellis or in a hanging container. Thunbergias prefer at least 4 hours of direct sunlight a day and cool nights. Keep the soil moist, and fertilize every other week during the fall and winter.

TRAILING VELVET PLANT: See **RUELLIA**

TROPAEOLUM: More commonly called nasturtiums, these are annuals that will flower most of the winter. They produce fragrant 2-inch blooms in a wide range of colors. Some varieties are bushy, growing up to 2 feet high, while trailing types grow well in hanging containers. Nasturtiums require at least 4 hours of direct sunlight a day and prefer very cool nights. Keep the soil moist, and fertilize once a month.

TULIP: Tulips grow in a very wide range of colors and reach up to 3 feet high depending on variety. The flowers can be up to 7 inches across. They do best in indirect sunlight and prefer very cool nights. Keep the soil moist, and do not fertilize.

TURK'S CAP: See **MALVAVISCUS**

TWELVE APOSTLES: See **NEOMARICA**

VALLOTA: Also known as Scarborough lily, this plant produces clusters of scarlet flowers on top of 2-foot-high stalks. They require at least 4 hours of direct sunlight a day and prefer fairly cool nights. Keep the soil moist, and fertilize once a month during the spring, summer, and fall. Do not feed after the flowers have faded.

WAX BEGONIA: See **BEGONIA**

WAX PLANT: See **HOYA**

WIDOW'S TEAR: See **ACHIMENES**

ZANTEDESCHIA: Also known as calla lily, these plants produce waxy-looking, rolled single petals called spathes. Inside the spathe is a small spike bearing the tiny true flower of the plant. Calla lilies prefer direct sunlight, but should be partially shaded from the midday sun. They prefer cool nights. Keep the soil very moist and fertilize once a month during the growing season.

ZEPHYR LILY: See **ZEPHYRANTHES**

ZEPHYRANTHES: Also known as the zephyr lily, these plants have 6-to-8-inch stalks, each producing a single 2-inch blossom of white, pink, or yellow. They prefer at least 4 hours of direct sunlight a day and very cool nights. Keep the soil moist, and fertilize once a month during the growing season. After the flowers and foliage wither, stop watering for about 10 weeks. Then resume watering and feeding.

14

INDOOR FOLIAGE PLANTS

Houseplants can be easily divided into two basic types: those that produce flowers (discussed in the previous chapter) and those that don't. Mention of a nonflowering houseplant would probably bring to mind a common green-leaved plant such as a philodendron for most people. But nonflowering, or foliage, plants come in a very wide variety of shapes, sizes, leaf patterns, and colors. The basic characteristic of a foliage houseplant is that the leaves or stems are attractive enough to provide pleasure without benefit of brightly colored flowers.

The advantage of foliage houseplants over the flowering types is that they are much better suited by nature to the light and temperatures found in the typical home. Foliage plants generally require neither the bright sunlight nor the cool night temperatures that their flowering brethren need to flourish. This is not to say that foliage plants do not prefer and respond to sunlight. They will grow bigger and faster in brighter light, but will tolerate and do well in lower light levels that a flowering plant could not tolerate. In addition, foliage plants typically do not go through alternating periods of blossoming and dormancy. They maintain their appearance year round.

BUYING NEW PLANTS

In buying a foliage houseplant, first check to see that the lower leaves are not pale or yellow and that none of the leaves have brown edges. Also make sure that the leaves are not too far apart, leaving gaps along the stem or branches. This is a sign that artificial means were used to stimulate too much growth too fast. The gaps will not fill in over time, and the plant will always look sparse. Check to see that the plant is not root bound. If it is, small root shoots will be showing above the soil or through the drainage holes in the bottom of the pot. Such overcrowding also shows up as newer leaves much smaller than the older growth.

Put a new plant in the sink and flush out the soil to remove any traces of excess fertilizing. Fill the pot with as much water as it will hold, let stand for an hour, and repeat. Keep the plant a little moister than usual for the first few weeks, to let it adjust from a humid greenhouse to the drier climate of your house. Keep a new plant away from others already in your house until you are sure that it does not have any insects or diseases. Your home is probably darker than the greenhouse where the plant was raised, and it is normal for a plant to drop a few leaves in adjusting to its new environment.

LIGHT

Remember that plants grow toward the light. If a plant is situated near a window, the side away from the window will tend to grow toward the light. To encourage even growth, rotate the plant ¼ turn regularly, such as once a week. The amount of light that you want a plant to get is a compromise between too little for the plant to live and so much that the plant grows too big too fast. In general, if the newer leaves are getting farther apart, the plant is not getting enough light and is stretching out for more. Too much light causes leaves to wilt during the heat of the day, and even turn brown.

If the plant is not getting enough light, move it closer to the window, move it to a sunnier part of the house, or use artificial lights to aid growth. Any artificial light will supplement sunlight and help a plant, but special fluorescent lights specifically designed for plants work best. If the plant is getting too much light, move it away from the window or use curtains to cut the light, particularly during the brightest part of the day.

WATER

Many experts contend that more plants die of overwatering than of lack of water. Plant roots require air as well as water, and too much water can literally drown a plant. The first sign of overwatering is yellowing leaves at the base of the plant. Underwatering shows up as wilting leaves, particularly at the ends of the stems, followed by browning edges of the lower leaves.

The major cause of overwatering is poor drainage. Make sure that the pot or container that the plant is in allows excess water to drain out the bottom. Also remember that plants in plastic containers require much less water than similar plants in clay containers. The clay containers soak up and evaporate a good deal of the water, while all the water put into a plastic container gets to the plant.

It is best to water plants with warm water. This avoids shock to the plant, and the plant can use warm water more quickly and efficiently. The water should be warmer than room temperature, but not unpleasantly hot to the touch. If your water has a high level of chlorine, fill a pot and let it stand overnight so that the chlorine evaporates before watering the plants. Also avoid using excessively saline water, such as produced by some water softeners. If you have such a water softener, your outside hose connection usually bypasses the water softener. Bring water in from outside for your houseplants rather than using tap water.

FERTILIZER

Indoor foliage plants require relatively infrequent fertilizing. Frequent feeding often just makes the plant outgrow its place in the house. Fertilizer can also cause damage, particularly if the low light levels do not let the plant grow fast enough to assimilate the fertilizer. Wait about 6 months before feeding a new plant, and feed every 4 to 6 months after that. Use a commercial fertilizer designed for houseplants, such as a 5–10–5 formulation. You can generally use a weaker application than that recommended by the manufacturer. Never apply more than called for on the label.

PROPAGATION

While the easiest way to get new plants is to buy them from the nursery, there is a lot of satisfaction in propagating your own at home. The method, as well as the ease of propagation, varies from plant to plant. Some plants are easy to propagate at home, and others are nearly impossible.

Propagation by division involves splitting a plant into two or more parts and replanting the parts as separate plants. This can be done with just about any plant that has two or more stems coming out of the soil. Division for most plants is best done in the spring. Simply remove the plant from its pot and pull it apart with your hands. You may have to cut apart the root ball with a knife. Repot the division immediately, keeping the soil moist and avoiding direct sunlight until the plant is established. Many plants send out runners that take root in the soil at the base of the main plant. These can be repotted in the same way as divided plants.

Many plants are propagated through stem or leaf cuttings. For stem cuttings, cut the end of a branch just below a leaf joint or node. Put the cutting in a moist rooting medium such as a mixture of 1 part sand and 2 parts peat moss in a clear plastic bag. Close the bag and put it in bright but not direct sunlight. When the shoots are an inch, open the bag and roll down the sides. After about a week, repot into containers.

SUCCULENTS

Succulents are leafless plants that store water in their stems. While most succulents are cacti, there are thousands of other plants, such as aloes, with the same characteristics. Cacti and other succulents are essentially desert plants, and therefore do very well in the low humidity of modern homes. Particular care should be taken to avoid overwatering cacti and other succulents. They certainly do not require as much water as other plants in your home. Cacti have an active growing season lasting from spring through early fall. During this time, allow the soil to dry out between waterings. During the winter dormant period, water only every few weeks. Other succulents will require a little more water than cacti. Always try to water on a dry, sunny day, preferably in the morning. Sunlight stimulates the plant's water intake, while evaporating any excess water. Be sure to use warm water, warmer than room temperature but not hot.

On the other hand, being desert plants, these plants require a lot of sunlight. Cacti should be placed by a window on the sunniest side of the house. They can be moved outdoors in the summer, but should not be exposed to full sunlight during the hottest part of the day, as growing indoors will have weakened their ability to withstand the direct sun.

While these plants generally do well at normal household temperatures, cacti require cooler nights during the winter dormant period to bear flowers. As long as the temperature is above freezing, the cacti will do well and eventually blossom.

COMMON FOLIAGE HOUSEPLANTS

ACALYPHA: Acalyphas are tall, bushy plants, growing up to 6 feet high. The copperleaf variety has red- and copper-colored leaves. The plants are usually pruned to a height of about 3 feet. They do best with at least 4 hours of direct sunlight a day, but the light can be supplemented artificially so that they get at least 12 hours of total light per day. Acalyphas prefer relatively constant temperatures and do well in higher humidity. Plant in a mixture of equal parts loam, sand, and peat moss. Keep the soil slightly moist at all times, and feed with a commercial 5–10–5 fertilizer. Propagate from stem cuttings at any time, although late spring to early summer is best.

ACORUS: Also called the Japanese sweet flag, this plant produces long, grasslike leaves and grows up to a foot high. These plants do best in indirect sunlight and prefer cooler nights. Keep the soil very moist at all times. Plant in a mixture of equal parts sand, loam, and peat moss, and feed with a commercial 5–10–5 fertilizer. Propagate by root division at any time.

ADIANTUM: These are different varieties of maidenhair ferns. Depending on type, they can grow up to 2 feet tall. They do best in indirect light and prefer slightly cool nights. Maidenhead ferns grow best in relatively high humidity. Keep the soil wet during the growing season, cutting back on the water during the winter. Do not feed newly potted plants for about 6 months. After that, feed twice a year with a standard commercial fertilizer. Plant in an equal mixture of sand, peat moss, loam, and fir bark. Propagate by root division in the late winter.

ADROMISCHUS: These are succulents with clumps of thick leaves and practically no stems. They do best with at least 4 hours of direct sunlight a day and prefer cool nights. Allow the soil to dry between waterings during the growing season. In winter, water only enough to prevent wilting. Do not feed during the first year, and then fertilize once a year. Plant in a mixture of equal parts potting soil and sand. Propagate from leaf cuttings at any time.

AGAVE: Also known as century plants, these succulents have sword-shaped leaves with sharp tips. Most species of century plant are too large for use as houseplants, but some, because of their very slow growth, can be grown indoors for many years before they outgrow their surroundings. Century plants require at least 4 hours of direct sunlight a day, or 12 hours of artificial light. They prefer cool nights. Allow the soil to dry between waterings in the growing season, and water in the winter only enough to prevent wilting. Do not feed new plants for the first year, and then fertilize every spring with a diluted commercial fertilizer. Plant in a mixture of equal parts potting soil and sand.

AGLAONEMA: Also known as Chinese evergreens, these plants can grow up to 2 feet high and do well in low light situations. They prefer constant and warm temperatures. Keep the soil moist, and do not feed for the first 6 months. Once the plants are established, feed every 3 to 4 months with a commercial 5–10–5 fertilizer. Plant in a mixture of equal parts loam, peat moss, and sand. Chinese evergreens can be propagated from stem cuttings at any time.

ALGERIAN IVY: See **HEDERA**

ALOE: Aloes are succulents that grow rosettes of leaves and often produce clusters of small flowers in winter. Height varies with species, with true aloe growing up to 2 feet high. Aloe ointment is made from the juice of the true aloe plant. Aloes need at least 4 hours of direct sunlight a day, or 12 hours of artificial light. They prefer cool nights. Allow the soil to dry between waterings, and do not feed the first year.

Once established, plants should be fed once a year in the fall, using a diluted commercial fertilizer. Plant in a mixture of equal parts potting soil and sand, adding limestone and bone meal. Aloes can be propagated from the young shoots that grow around the base of the plant.

ARAUCARIA: Also known as Norfolk Island pine, this plant grows slowly (4 to 5 inches a year) and has pinelike needles. These plants do best in indirect sunlight and prefer cool nights. Keep the soil moist but not wet. Do not feed for the first 6 months, and then fertilize every 4 months using a commercial 5–10–5 fertilizer. It is very difficult to propagate these plants at home.

ASPARAGUS: Ornamental asparagus ferns are easy-to-grow houseplants that reach up to 2 feet high. Cut stems are often added to floral arrangements as greenery. They do best in indirect sunlight and can be grown under artificial lights. They prefer cool nights. Keep the soil moist but not wet. Do not feed for the first 6 months, and then feed every 3 to 4 months with a commercial fertilizer. Plant in a mixture of equal parts loam, peat moss, and sand. Propagate at any time by root division.

ASPIDISTRA: Also known as the cast-iron plant for its ability to tolerate a wide variety of conditions unfavorable to other plants. It grows to about 3 feet high, with wide arching leaves. Aspidistras do best in indirect sunlight and prefer cool nights. Keep the soil moist, and feed monthly during the growing season. Do not feed from late fall to early spring. Plant in a mixture of equal parts loam, peat moss, and sand. Propagate in early spring by root division.

ASPLENIUM: Varieties of this plant are known as bird's nest fern and mother fern. All are also called spleenwort. Spleenworts have long fronds that grow up to 15 inches high. They do best in indirect sunlight, but can be grown under artificial light. They prefer cooler nights and relatively high humidity, although the bird's nest fern will tolerate drier air than the other varieties. Keep the soil moist from midspring to midfall, drier the rest of the year. Do not feed spleenworts for the first 6 months, and fertilize every 6 months after that with a diluted commercial fertilizer. Plant in a mixture of equal parts sand, peat moss, loam, and fir bark.

BALL CACTUS: See NOTOCACTUS

BALL FERN: See DAVALLIA

BEAUCARNEA: Also called the elephant-foot tree, this plant is characterized by the large bulbous swelling of the trunk at soil level and wrinkled brownish bark resembling elephant skin. It requires little care and can grow up to 30 feet tall. The elephant-foot tree requires at least 4 hours of direct sunlight a day or over 12 hours of artificial light. They prefer cool nights, but can tolerate a wide range of temperatures. Allow the soil to dry between waterings. Do not feed new plants, and then feed once a year in the spring. Plant in a mixture of equal parts loam, peat moss, and sand. Propagate from seed at any time.

BEGONIA: There are three major classes of begonias grown as houseplants: rex begonia, rhizomatous begonia, and basket begonia. Rex begonias have bright foliage, with a variety of colors blended into the green leaves, and trailing stems. Rhizomatous begonias have thick succulent stems. They grow up to a foot or more high and up to 2 feet across. Basket begonias have trailing stems and do well in hanging containers.

Begonias do best in indirect sunlight, but should have at least 4 hours of direct sunlight in winter in northern areas. Keep the soil barely moist, as begonias are very susceptible to damage from overwatering. Feed every other month from midwinter to late fall with a diluted commercial fertilizer. Do not feed the rest of the year. Plant in a mixture of equal parts peat moss, sand, loam, and vermiculite, adding limestone and bone meal.

BEGONIA TREEBINE: See **CISSUS**

BIRD'S NEST FERN: See **ASPLENIUM**

BOSTON FERN: See **NEPHROLEPIS**

BOXWOOD: See **BUXUS**

BRASSAIA: Also known as scheffleras, these plants can grow to 6 feet high, with foot-long leaves when mature. Scheffleras require at least 4 hours of direct sunlight a day, or over 12 hours of artificial light. Allow the soil to dry between waterings. Do not feed for the first 6 months, and feed every 6 months after that. Plant in a mixture of equal parts loam, peat moss, and sand. Propagate from seed at any time.

BURRO'S TAIL: See **SEDUM**

BUTTERFLY PALM: See **CHRYSALIDOCARPUS**

BUXUS: Also known as boxwood, these plants have long been grown as outdoor evergreens. They have 1-inch shiny leaves that respond well to shearing and can be shaped as desired. They can grow to over 4 feet high, but are usually trained as miniature trees. Boxwoods require at least 4 hours a day of direct sunlight, or over 12 hours of artificial light. They prefer very cool nights. Keep the soil barely moist. Do not feed for the first year. After that feed once a year in the spring, using a commercial fertilizer. Plant in a mixture of equal parts sand, loam, and peat moss. Propagate from stem cuttings in late summer.

CALADIUM: Caladiums have large, colorful leaves that grow up to 2 feet long. The plants grow from large tubers and go dormant for 4 to 5 months. Caladiums do best in indirect sunlight, but can be grown under artificial lights. Keep the soil moist during the growing season, and feed every other week. Plant in a mixture of 2 parts loam, 2 parts peat moss, 1 part sand, and 1 part dried manure.

Propagate by dividing the tubers. After the foliage withers, stop watering, remove and clean the tubers, and store in dry peat moss for 4 to 5 months, and then replant.

CALATHEA: Also known as the peacock plant, calatheas have red stalks and green leaves with red and purple undersides. Peacock plants do best in indirect sunlight and prefer high humidity. Keep the soil very moist, and feed every other week with a commercial fertilizer. Plant in a mixture of equal parts peat moss, sand, vermiculite, and dried manure.

CALLISIA: This plant has inch-long green-and-white-striped leaves with purple undersides. It is usually grown in hanging containers. It does best in indirect sunlight, but can be grown under artificial lights. Keep the soil moist. Do not feed for the first 6 months, and then fertilize every 4 months. Plant in a mixture of equal parts of loam, peat moss, and sand. Propagate from stem cuttings at any time.

CARYOTA: Also called the tufted fishtail palm, this tree-like plant can grow up to 5 feet high. It should not be pruned and will eventually grow too large for indoors. Fishtail palms do best in indirect sunlight, but can be grown under artificial lights. Keep the soil very moist at all times. Feed once a month from spring to fall, and do not feed the rest of the year. Plant in a mixture of equal parts loam, sand, peat moss, and dried manure. Propagate at any time from seed or from the suckers that grow at the base of the plant.

CAST-IRON PLANT: See **ASPIDISTRA**

CENTURY PLANT: See **AGAVE**

CEPHALOCEREUS: Also known as old man cactus, these plants have a single upright stem about a foot high and are covered with long bristles resembling hair. These cacti do best with at least 4 hours of direct sunlight a day, but can be grown under artificial lights. They prefer cool nights and can tolerate heat. Allow the soil to dry between waterings. Do not feed the first year. After that, fertilize once a year in the spring. Plant in a mixture of equal parts sand and potting soil, adding limestone and bone meal. Propagate at any time from stem cuttings.

CEROPEGIA: Also known as rosary vines, these plants have trailing stems that grow up to 3 feet long. The small leaves are green with silverish tops and purple undersides. They are usually grown in hanging containers. Rosary vines grow best in indirect sunlight and can be grown in artificial light. They prefer cool nights. Allow the soil to dry between waterings from spring to fall. Water only enough in winter to prevent wilting. Feed every other month in spring and summer, using a diluted commercial fertilizer, and do not feed the rest of the year. Plant in a mixture of equal parts potting soil and sand, adding limestone and bone meal. Propagate at any time from stem cuttings.

CHAMAEDOREA: Also known as parlor palm, this is a dwarf species able to live in cramped quarters. It will grow up to 18 inches high and has fronds up to a foot long. Parlor palms grow best in indirect light and can be grown under artificial light. Keep the soil moist. Fertilize from early spring to early fall, and do not feed the rest of the year. Plant in a mixture of equal parts sand, loam, peat moss, and dried manure, adding bone meal. Propagate from seeds at any time.

CHAMAEROPS: More commonly known as the European fan palm, this plant grows up to 6 feet high with stiff leaves about 18 inches long. The leaves grow from rough stems with black hairlike coverings. European fan palms do best with at least 4 hours of direct sunlight a day, but can be grown with over 12 hours of artificial light daily. Keep the soil very moist. They prefer cool nights and should be fed monthly from early spring to early fall. Do not feed the rest of the year. Plant in a mixture of equal parts loam, peat moss, sand, and dried manure. Propagate at any time from seed or from the suckers that grow at the base of the plant.

CHINESE EVERGREEN: See **AGLAONEMA**

CHINESE FAN PALM: See **LIVISTONA**

CHINESE PODOCARPUS: See **PODOCARPUS**

CHINESE RUBBER PLANT: See **CRASSULA**

CHLOROPHYTUM: Also known as the spider plant, chlorophytum has grasslike long green leaves growing up to 16 inches long. The leaves are usually striped with white or yellow. Spider plants do best in indirect sunlight and can be grown under artificial light. Keep the soil moist at all times. They prefer cool nights and should not be fed in the first 6 months. After that, feed every 4 months with a commercial fertilizer. Plant in a mixture of equal parts loam, peatmoss, and sand. Propagate at any time by root division.

CHRYSALIDOCARPUS: Also known as the butterfly palm, these plants grow up to 5 feet high, producing 3-foot fronds. They cannot be pruned and may grow too large for indoors. Butterfly palms do best in indirect sunlight and can be grown under artificial light. Keep the soil very moist. These plants prefer constant temperatures and should be fed monthly from spring to fall. Plant in a mixture of equal parts loam, sand, peat moss, and dried manure. Propagate from seeds at any time.

CIBOTIUM: These plants are also known as Hawaiian and Mexican tree ferns. They grow up to 6 feet across and can grow up to 8 feet high. They do best in indirect sunlight and can be grown under artificial lights. They prefer cool nights. Keep the soil barely moist. Do not feed for the first 6 months, feeding every 6 months after that, using a diluted commercial fertilizer. Plant in a mixture of equal parts potting soil and peat moss, adding bone meal.

CISSUS: Various types are called grape ivy, kangaroo ivy, and begonia treebine. The plants cling to supports with grapelike tendrils, but can also be grown in hanging containers. These plants prefer indirect sunlight, but can be grown under artificial lights. They prefer cool nights and high humidity. Allow the soil to dry between waterings. Do not feed for the first 6 months, and then feed every 4 months with a commercial fertilizer. Plant in a mixture of equal parts loam, sand, and peat moss. Propagate from stem cuttings at any time.

CODIAEUM: Also known as croton, these plants come in a wide variety of colors and leaf patterns. Leaf colors include yellow, red, copper, pink, and orange. They tend to grow into bushy plants up to 5 feet high if not pruned. Crotons prefer at least 4 hours of direct sunlight a day, but can be grown under 12 or more hours of artificial light. They prefer constant temperatures and should be kept out of drafts. Keep the soil barely moist. Feed every other month from early spring to midsummer, and do not feed the rest of the year. Plant in a mixture of equal parts loam, peat moss, and sand. Propagate in the spring from stem cuttings.

COLEUS: Coleuses grow 2 to 3 feet high, with 4-inch leaves combining many shades of green, yellow, pink, and red. They do best in at least 4 hours of direct sunlight a day, but can be grown in 12 hours or more of artificial light. Keep the soil barely moist. Do not feed for the first 6 months, and then feed every 3 months with a diluted commercial fertilizer. Plant in a mixture of equal parts loam, sand, and peat moss. Propagate from stem cuttings at any time.

CORDYLINE: Also known as the Hawaiian ti plant, these require very high humidity and can grow up to 6 feet high. The leaves are pink and green or pink, red, and white, depending on species. Hawaiian ti plants require at least 4 hours of direct sunlight a day for full color, but can be grown under artificial light. They prefer constant temperatures. Do not feed for the first 6 months, and then feed every 4 months with a commercial fertilizer. Plant in a mixture of equal parts loam, peat moss, and sand. Propagate at any time from stem cuttings.

COSTUS: The two main species of costus are known as spiral flag and stepladder plant. Both grow up to 3 feet high and may occasionally produce small flowers. The stepladder plant has oval green leaves about a foot long, while the spiral flag has 4-inch pointed green leaves with silvery central ribs. These plants do best in indirect sunlight and can be grown in artificial light. Keep the soil moist, and do not feed for the first 6 months. After that, feed every 4 months with a commercial fertilizer. Plant in a mixture of equal parts loam, peat moss, and sand, or use a potting soil. Propagate by root division in paring, or by stem cuttings at any time.

CRASSULA: One major species is known as the silver dollar plant, the other is called either the jade plant or the Chinese rubber plant. They grow up to 30 inches high and have smooth oval, red-edged leaves. These plants do best with at least 4 hours of direct sunlight a day, but can be grown under at least 12 hours of artificial light daily. They prefer cool nights, but can tolerate a wide range of temperatures. Allow the soil to dry between waterings. Do not feed for the first 6 months, and then feed every 4 months with a commercial fertilizer. Plant in a mixture of equal parts loam, peat moss, and sand. Propagate at any time from stem cuttings.

CROTON: See **CODIAEUM**

CYATHEA: Also known as the tree fern, this plant is native to Puerto Rico, where it can grow up to 50 feet high in the wild. Its growth slows indoors, producing 2-foot-long fronds after 5 years or more. Tree ferns do best in indirect sunlight and prefer cool nights. Keep the soil very moist. Do not feed for the first 6 months, and feed every six months after that with a diluted commercial fertilizer. Plant in a mixture of equal parts loam, peat moss, fir bark, and sand.

CYCAS: The two most common species are the fern palm and the sago palm. They have leathery leaves that resemble fern fronds, growing up to 2 feet long. They do best in indirect sunlight and prefer cool nights. Allow the soil to dry between waterings. Feed every other month from early spring to midsummer, and do not feed the rest of the year. Plant in a mixture of equal parts loam, peat moss, and sand. Propagate at any time from the seeds or from the suckers that grow at the base of the plant.

CYPERUS: Also known as the umbrella plant, these grow up to 4 feet high, with 5-to-7-inch leaves on top of slender stalks. They do best with at least 4 hours of direct sunlight a day, but can be grown with 12 or more hours of artificial light daily. Keep the soil wet at all times. Fertilize once a week from early spring to late summer with a diluted commercial fertilizer. Plant in a mixture of equal parts loam, peat moss, and sand. Propagate at any time from seeds or by root division.

CYRTOMIUM: Also known as holly ferns, these plants are very tolerant of low light and low humidity. They grow up to 2 feet high, with 3-to-5-inch leaves. Holly ferns do well in indirect light and can be grown in artificial light. Keep the soil barely moist at all times. Do not feed for the first 6 months, and then feed every 6 months with a diluted commercial fertilizer. Plant in a mixture of equal parts loam, sand, peat moss, and fir bark.

DAVALLIA: Various species of davallia include deer's foot fern, rabbit's foot fern, squirrel's foot fern, and ball fern. All have creeping stems covered with coarse hairlike growth. These plants are well suited for hanging containers, and most grow to 12 to 18 inches high. Davallias do best in shaded light and can be grown in artificial light. Keep the soil barely moist at all times. Do not feed for the first 6 months, and then feed every 6 months with a diluted commercial fertilizer. Plant in a mixture of equal parts loam, sand, fir bark, and peat moss.

DEER'S FOOT FERN: See **DAVALLIA**

DEVIL'S BACKBONE: See **PEDILANTHUS**

DEVIL'S IVY: See **SCINDAPSUS**

DIEFFENBACHIA: These plants grow up to 5 feet high, with broad leaves up to 18 inches long. The leaves and stems are poisonous and should be kept away from children and pets. Dieffenbachia do best in indirect sunlight and can be grown in artificial light. Allow the soil to dry between waterings. Do not feed for the first 4 months, and then feed every other month with a diluted commercial fertilizer. Plant in a mixture of equal parts loam, peat moss, and sand. Cut the plants back in the spring to stimulate growth. Propagate at any time from stem cuttings.

DRACAENA: Dracaenas come in a very wide variety of shapes and colors, many of which bear absolutely no resemblance to one another. The dragon tree has thick pointed leaves up to 2 feet long, while the gold dust dracaena grows to about 2 feet high and has 2-inch oval leaves. Dracaenas do best in indirect sunlight and can be grown in artificial light. Keep the soil moist at all times. Do not feed for the first 6 months. After that, feed every 6 months. Plant in a mixture of equal parts loam, sand, and peat moss. Propagate from stem cuttings at any time.

ECHEVERIA: Species include painted lady and Mexican snowball. Echeverias are succulents, with rosettes of low leaves. Most grow 2 to 4 inches across, although some species can grow over a foot high. They do best with at least 4 hours of direct sunlight a day, but can be grown with 12 hours or more of artificial light. Allow the soil to dry between waterings from spring to fall, and water in winter only enough to prevent wilting. Do not feed the first year. After that, feed once a year in the spring, using a diluted commercial fertilizer. Plant in a mixture of equal parts potting soil and sand. Propagate at any time with stem cuttings.

ELEPHANT-FOOT TREE: See **BEAUCARNEA**

ENGLISH IVY: See **HEDERA**

EUONYMUS: There are two types generally grown as houseplants, the winter creeper and the evergreen euonymus. The winter creeper is a climbing plant with 18-inch stems and white-edged green leaves. The evergreen euonymus grows up to 3 feet high and has bright green leaves. They do best in indirect sunlight and can be grown under artificial lights. Keep the soil barely moist. They prefer cool nights and can tolerate very cool temperatures. Do not feed for the first 6 months, and then feed every 4 months. Plant in a commercial potting-soil mixture. Propagate at any time from stem cuttings.

EUPHORBIA: There are over 1,600 species of euphorbia, including the poinsettia so popular at Christmas. Others are succulents closely resembling cacti. The succulents do produce flowers, which are short-lived and contain an acidic sap that is highly irritating. The succulents can grow up to 3 feet or more. They do best with at least 4 hours of direct sunlight a day, but can be grown under artificial light of over 12 hours daily. They prefer cool nights and warm days. Allow the soil to dry between waterings from spring to fall, and water in the winter only enough to prevent wilting. Plant in a mixture of equal parts potting soil and sand. Propagate in spring or summer from stem cuttings.

EUROPEAN FAN PALM: See **CHAMAEROPS**

FALSE HOLLY: See **OSMANTHUS**

FATSHEDERA: Also known as tree ivy, this is a viny shrub that can grow up to 10 inches across and 3 feet high. It does best with at least 4 hours of direct sunlight a day, but can be grown under artificial lights. They prefer cool nights and can tolerate very cool temperatures. Do not feed for the first 6 months, and then feed every 4 months. Plant in a mixture of equal parts loam, peatmoss, and sand. Propagate at any time from stem cut-tings.

FATSIA: More commonly known as the Japanese fatsia, this plant has deeply cut leaves that grow up to 16 inches across. The plant can reach up to 4 feet high, but can be pruned as desired. It does best with at least 4 hours of direct sunlight a day, but can be grown with over 12 hours of artificial light daily. Keep the soil barely moist. Do not feed for the first 6 months. After that, feed twice a year in spring and summer. Plant in a mixture of equal parts loam, peat moss, and sand. Propagate in early spring from the suckers that grow at the base of the plant.

FERN PALM: See **CYCAS**

FICUS: The most common variety is the Indian rubber tree, which has dark green oval leaves that grow up to 10 inches long. They are usually sold as 2-to-3-foot-high plants and can eventually reach 8 feet high. As houseplants, they should be pruned before reaching the ceiling. They do best in indirect sunlight and prefer constant temperatures. Keep the soil barely moist. Do not feed for the first 6 months. After that, feed twice a year. Plant in a mixture of equal parts loam, peat moss, and sand.

FITTONIA: Fittonias are creeping plants, growing up to 8 inches long with 2-to-4-inch green leaves with prominent veins. They require a very warm, humid growing environ-ment. Fittonias do best in indirect sunlight and can be grown under artificial lights. They grow best in the high humidity of a terrarium and prefer constant temperatures. Keep the soil moist at all times. Do not feed for the first 4 months, and then feed once a month with a diluted commercial fertilizer. Plant in standard potting soil. Propagate from stem cuttings in spring or summer.

GASTERIA: Gasterias are succulents with white-spotted, tongue-shaped leaves. They grow up to 8 inches high, depending on species. Gasterias grow best in bright indirect sunlight, but can be grown in artificial light. They prefer cool nights. Allow the soil to dry between waterings. Do not feed for the first year, and after that feed in the spring with a diluted commercial fertilizer. Plant in a mixture of equal parts potting soil and sand. Propagate at any time from the suckers that grow at the base of the plant.

GERMAN IVY: See **SENECIO**

GOLDEN POLYPODY FERN: See **POLYPODIUM**

GOLDEN POTHOS: See **SCINDAPSUS**

GOLDEN STAR CACTUS: See **MAMMILLARIA**

GRAPE IVY: See **CISSUS**

GREVILLEA: Also known as the silk oak tree, grevillea has leaves up to 18 inches long that strongly resemble fern fronds. They grow very rapidly, up to a foot a year. Silk oaks do best with at least 4 hours of direct sunlight a day, but can be grown with 12 or more hours of artificial light daily. Allow the soil to dry between waterings. Do not feed for the first 4 months, and then feed every 3 months. Plant in a mixture of equal parts loam, peat moss, and sand. Prune the branches back in the spring to keep the plant small enough for the house.

GYNURA: Gynuras have dark green, 3-to-4-inch leaves with velvety purple hairs. They occasionally produce small orange flowers and are usually grown in hanging containers. Gynuras do best with at least 4 hours of direct sunlight a day, but they can be grown under artificial light. Keep the soil barely moist at all times. Do not feed for the first 4 months, and then feed once a month with a diluted commercial fertilizer. Plant in potting soil. Pinch back the branch tips to encourage dense growth. Propagate by planting the pinched tips.

HAWAIIAN TI PLANT: See **CORDYLINE**

HAWAIIAN TREE FERN: See **CIBOTIUM**

HAWORTHIA: Haworthias are succulents that form small rosettes of leaves that curve upward as they grow. The leaves have patterns of wartlike ridges, some resembling zebra stripes. These plants are very easy to grow. They do best in indirect sunlight and can be grown under artificial light. Allow the soil to dry between waterings. Do not feed for the first year. After that, feed once a year in the spring with a diluted commercial fertilizer. Plant in a mixture of equal parts potting soil and sand. Propagate from the suckers that grow around the base of the plant.

HEDERA: The two major species are also known as English ivy and Algerian ivy. These plants produce climbing vines that cling to almost any surface. In the home, they are usually planted in hanging containers with the vines trailing over the sides, although they can also be trained to grow on a trellis. These ivies do best with at least 4 hours of direct sunlight a day. They prefer cool nights, and English ivy can tolerate very cool temperatures. Do not feed for the first 4 months, and then feed every 3 months. Plant in potting soil. Pinch back the stems to encourage bushy growth. Propagate by planting the pinched-off stems.

HOLLY FERN: See **CYRTOMIUM**

HOWEA: Howeas include the sentry palm and the thatch-leaf palm. These are among the best-suited palms for indoor growing because of their slow growth rate, but they will eventually grow too tall for the house. They have long arching leaves growing from a single trunk. They do best in indirect sunlight and fairly constant temperatures. Keep the soil barely moist at all times. Do not feed during the first 6 months. After that, feed once a month from early spring to early fall and not at all the rest of the year. Plant in potting soil with a high content of organic matter. Propagate from seeds at any time.

HYPOESTES: Also known as the pink polka dot, this plant has 2-inch leaves that are hairy and have pink spots. It grows up to a foot tall, and just as wide. These plants do best in indirect sunlight and constant temperatures. Keep the soil barely moist at all times and do not fertilize. Plant in a potting mixture with a high content of organic matter. Propagate from stem cuttings at any time.

INDIAN RUBBER TREE: See **FICUS**

INDOOR OAK: See **NICODEMIA**

JADE PLANT: See **CRASSULA**

JAPANESE FATSIA: See **FATSIA**

JAPANESE SWEET FLAG: See **ACORUS**

KALANCHOE: Kalanchoes are succulents that are easy to grow and have green leaves with reddish-purple blotches. They can grow over a foot high and occasionally produce small flowers. Kalanchoes do best with at least 4 hours of direct sunlight a day, but can be grown with 12 hours or more of artificial light daily. Allow the soil to dry between waterings. Do not feed for the first 6 months, and then feed every 6 months. Plant in a mixture of equal parts potting soil and sand. Propagate from stem cuttings at any time.

KANGAROO IVY: See **CISSUS**

LADY FERN: See **RHAPIS**

LAUREL: See **LAURUS**

LAURUS: Also known as laurel or sweet bay, its leaves are used for seasoning in cooking. Laurel can grow fairly tall, and is usually pruned to keep it under 4 feet high. Laurels do best with at least 4 hours of direct sunlight a day, but can be grown in 12 hours or more of artificial light daily. Keep the soil barely moist at all times. Do not feed for the first 6 months. After that, feed every other month from early spring to midsummer, and not at all the rest of the year. Plant in potting soil and propagate at any time from stem cuttings.

LINGUSTRUM: Also known as the Texas privet, this plant grows up to 6 feet high with large waxy leaves. It is very hardy and tolerates cool drafts well. Privets do best with at least 4 hours of direct sunlight a day, but can be grown with at least 12 hours of artificial light daily. Keep the soil barely moist at all times. Do not feed during the first 6 months, and then feed every other month from early spring to midsummer and not at all the rest of the year. Plant in potting soil, and prune during spring or summer. Propagate at any time from stem cuttings.

LIVISTONA: Also known as the Chinese fan palm, the livistona produces long leaves in a fan shape up to 18 inches across. Fan palms do best in bright indirect sunlight and can be grown under artificial light. Keep the soil wet at all times. Do not feed new plants until spring and then feed once a month from spring to early fall and not at all the rest of the year. Plant in a potting soil with a high content of organic matter. Propagate at any time from seeds.

MAMMILLARIA: These cacti include the powder-puff cactus, the snowball pincushion, and the golden star cactus. They bear flowers in spring and winter and do well as small windowsill plants. These cacti do best with at least 4 hours of direct sunlight a day, but can be grown with 12 hours or more of artificial light daily. They prefer very cool nights and warm days. Allow the soil to dry between waterings from spring to fall, and water in the winter only enough to prevent wilting. Plant in a mixture of equal parts potting soil and sand. Propagate at any time from the small new plants that grow at the base of the plant.

MARANTA: Also known as the prayer plant or the arrow-root, this plant has broad leaves that are horizontal in the light and turn vertical in the dark. They do best in indirect sunlight and can be grown in artificial light. Keep the soil moist from spring to fall, allowing it to dry between waterings in winter. Plant in potting soil. Do not feed during the first 4 months or during the winter, and feed every other month the rest of the year.

MEXICAN SNOWBALL: See ECHEVERIA

MEXICAN TREE FERN: See CIBOTIUM

MINIATURE DATE PALM: See PHOENIX

MONSTERA: Monsteras grow wild as jungle vines in Central America. They have large leaves, up to a foot long, with deeply cut lobes. The plants will eventually reach ceiling height, at which time they should be discarded. Monsteras do best in indirect sunlight, but can be grown under artificial light. They prefer fairly constant temperatures, but will tolerate cool nights. Keep the soil barely moist at all times. Do not feed for the first 6 months, and then feed twice a year in early spring and early summer. Plant in potting soil. Propagate at any time from stem cuttings.

MOTHER FERN: See ASPLENIUM

MOTHER-IN-LAW TONGUE: See SANSEVIERIA

MYRTLE: See MYRTUS

MYRTUS: More commonly called myrtle, this is a popular garden plant whose dwarf variety makes a good houseplant. It grows up to 4 feet high, and up to 3 to 4 feet across. It produces ½-inch leaves on long slender branches. Myrtles do best with at least 4 hours of direct sunlight a day, but can be grown with at least 12 hours of artificial light daily. They prefer cool nights and will tolerate a wide range of temperatures. Allow the soil to dry between waterings. Do not feed for the first 6 months or in winter. Feed every 3 months the rest of the year. Plant in potting soil, and prune in early spring to control the size. Propagate at any time from stem cuttings.

NEPHROLEPIS: Also known as the sword fern, the most common variety is the Boston fern. The Boston fern has arching fronds reaching up to 3 feet long and flat 3-inch leaves. Boston ferns do best in bright indirect light, but can be grown in artificial light. They prefer cool nights. Keep the soil barely moist at all times. Do not feed for the first 6 months, and then feed twice a year, in early spring and in midsummer. Plant in a mixture of equal parts potting soil and peat moss. Propagate by root division in the spring.

NICODEMIA: Also known as the indoor oak, this plant grows up to 18 inches high and has leaves resembling oak leaves. The plant is bushy and can be trained to be even bushier by pinching back new growth. Indoor oaks do best with at least 4 hours of direct sunlight a day, but can be grown in artificial light. Keep the soil barely moist at all times. Do not feed the first 3 months or in fall or winter. Feed every other week the rest of the year with a diluted commercial fertilizer. Plant in potting soil. Propagate from stem cuttings in spring or summer.

NORFOLK ISLAND PINE: See **ARAUCARIA**

NOTOCACTUS: More commonly called ball cactus, these cacti are ball-shaped when young, growing into a tall cylindrical shape as they age. They grow well on windowsills and produce yellow flowers. They do best with at least 4 hours of direct sunlight a day, but can be grown with at least 12 hours of artificial light daily. They prefer cooler nights, particularly in the winter. Allow the soil to dry between waterings from spring to fall, and water in the winter only enough to prevent wilting. Do not fertilize for the first year. After that, feed once a year in the spring. Plant in a mixture of equal parts potting soil and sand, adding limestone and bone meal. Propagate at any time from the young suckers that grow at the base of the plant.

OLD MAN CACTUS: See **CEPHALOCEREUS**

OLIVE: Olive trees can be grown as houseplants and can be pruned to keep the size manageable. The plant has leaves up to 3 inches long and occasionally produces very small white flowers. It will usually not produce fruit indoors due to the difficulty of pollination. Olive trees do best with at least 4 hours of direct sunlight a day, but can be grown under artificial light. They prefer very cool nights and will tolerate a very wide range of temperatures. Allow the soil to dry between waterings. Do not feed for the first 6 months. After that, feed twice a year in spring and summer. Plant in a mixture of equal parts loam, peat moss, and sand. Propagate at any time from stem cuttings.

OSMANTHUS: Also known as false holly, this plant grows up to 3 feet tall with 2-inch dark green leaves resembling holly leaves. The plants are very tolerant of cold and drafts. These plants do best with at least 4 hours of direct sunlight a day, but they can be grown under artificial light. Keep the soil barely moist at all times. Do not feed for the first 6 months. After that, feed twice a year, in early spring and early summer. Plant in potting soil. Prune plants in early spring to control size. Propagate at any time from stem cuttings.

PACHYPHYTUM: These are succulents that grow well as windowsill plants. One variety, known as silver bract, grows up to a foot high with thick gray-white leaves that curve upward. Pachyphytums do best with at least 4 hours of direct sunlight a day, and they prefer cool nights. Do not feed during the first year. After that, feed once a year in the spring with a diluted commercial fertilizer. Plant in a mixture of equal parts potting soil and sand, adding limestone and bone meal. Propagate at any time from stem cuttings.

PAINTED LADY: See **ECHEVERIA**

PANDANUS: Also known as the screw pine, this plant has sharp-edged leaves that grow up to 2 feet long and about 2 inches wide. It is not a pine tree, but does produce conelike fruit when grown outdoors. Screw pines grow best in indirect sunlight, but can be grown under artificial light. Allow the soil to dry between waterings. Do not feed for the first 6 months, and then feed every 3 months with a commercial fertilizer. Plant in potting soil. Propagate at any time from the suckers that grow around the base of the plant.

PARLOR PALM: See **CHAMAEDOREA**

PEACOCK PLANT: See **CALATHEA**

PEDILANTHUS: Commonly called the devil's backbone; the plant's leaves alternate along the stem in a zigzag effect. It grows up to 3 feet high, with 2-to-3-inch leaves. The stems produce a strong sap that can cause skin irritation. These plants do best in indirect sunlight and can be grown in artificial light. Keep the soil barely moist at all times. Do not feed for the first 6 months or in the fall or winter. Feed every other month the rest of the year. Plant in a mixture of equal parts loam, peat moss, and sand. Propagate from stem cuttings at any time.

PEPEROMIA: Peperomias have thick leaves and usually grow under a foot high. They produce taillike flower stalks in spring. They do best in bright indirect sunlight and can be grown under artificial light. Peperomias prefer fairly constant temperatures. Do not feed for the first 6 months. After that, feed every 3 months with a diluted commercial fertilizer. Plant in a mixture of equal parts loam, peat moss, and sand. Propagate at any time from stem cuttings.

PEPPER: Indoor peppers are pepper plants that provide the condiment used for seasoning and are not related to the bell or chile-pepper plants. These are vine plants that grow up to 4 to 5 feet high on a stake or trellis, or they can be grown in hanging containers. Peppers do best in bright indirect sunlight, but they can be grown in artificial light. They prefer fairly constant temperatures. Keep the soil barely moist at all times. Do not feed for the first 4 months, and then feed every other month. Plant in potting soil. Propagate at any time from stem cuttings.

PHILODENDRON: Philodendrons come from Central and South America, and there are over 200 varieties available. Most indoor varieties are vines, and are usually grown in hanging containers. The most popular is the heart-leaved philodendron, which has heart-shaped leaves 2 to 4 inches long. Philodendrons do best in indirect sunlight, but can be grown in artificial light. They generally prefer constant temperatures. Keep the soil barely moist at all times. Do not feed for the first 6 months, and feed every 3 months after that. Plant in a mixture of equal parts loam, peat moss, and sand. Propagate at any time from stem cuttings.

PHOENIX: Also called the miniature or pygmy date palm, these plants grow only to about 2 feet high and have arching leaves 1 to 2 feet long. Keep the soil very moist at all times. Do not feed new plants until their first spring, and then feed monthly during the spring and summer. Do not feed the rest of the year. Plant in a mixture of equal parts loam, peat moss, and sand, adding bone meal. Propagate at any time from seeds.

PIGGY-BACK PLANT: See **TOLMIEA**

PINK POLKA DOT: See **HYPOESTES**

PLATYCERIUM: More commonly known as the staghorn fern, this is an air-growing plant that sends its roots into tree bark rather than growing in soil. It is usually grown in a hanging container on bark-covered wood or on cork. Staghorn ferns do best in bright indirect light, but can be grown under artificial light. Keep the wood or other organic matter moist by soaking once a week in a sink or pail. Do not fertilize. Propagate at any time from the small shoots that grow at the bases of the fronds.

PLECTRANTHUS: Also called Swedish ivy, these plants have trailing stems up to 2 feet long with waxy leaves about an inch across. They do best in bright indirect sunlight, but can be grown in artificial light. Do not feed for the first 4 months, and feed every other month after that with a diluted commercial fertilizer. Plant in a mixture of equal parts loam, peat moss, and sand. Pinch back long stems to encourage dense growth. Propagate from stem cuttings at any time.

PODOCARPUS: More commonly called the Chinese podocarpus, this plant can grow up to 6 feet high, but is usually pruned to a more manageable height. It has dark green needlelike leaves about 3 inches long and ½ inch wide. These plants do best with at least 4 hours of direct sunlight a day, but can be grown under at least 12 hours of artificial light daily. They prefer cool nights and can tolerate warmer temperatures. Keep the soil barely moist. Do not feed during the first 6 months, and then feed twice a year in early spring and in early summer. Plant in a mixture of equal parts loam, peat moss, and sand. Prune in early spring before new growth begins. Propagate in the fall from stem cuttings.

POINSETTIA: See **EUPHORBIA**

POLYPODIUM: Also known as the golden polypody fern, this plant has leathery fronds up to 2 feet long. They do best in bright indirect sunlight and can be grown under artificial lights. Keep the soil barely moist. Do not feed during the first 6 months, and then feed twice a year with diluted commercial fertilizer. Plant in a mixture of equal parts loam, peat moss, sand, and fir bark, adding bone meal.

POWDER-PUFF CACTUS: See **MAMMILLARIA**

PRAYER PLANT: See **MARANTA**

PURPLE HEART: See **SETCREASEA**

PYGMY DATE PALM: See **PHOENIX**

RABBIT'S FOOT FERN: See **DAVALLIA**

RHAPIS: Also known as lady ferns, these plants produce clusters of wide leaves on slender stems that grow up to 5 feet high. They do best in bright indirect sunlight and can be grown under artificial lights. Keep the soil very moist. Plant in a potting soil with a high content of organic matter. Propagate at any time from the suckers that grow around the base of the plant.

RICE-PAPER PLANT: See **TETRAPANAX**

ROSARY VINE: See **CEROPEGIA**

SAGO PALM: See **CYCAS**

SANSEVIERIA: Also called snake plant or mother-in-law tongue, these plants have thick leaves 18 to 24 inches long that grow in rosettes from underground stems. The leaves have horizontal zigzag stripes. Sansevierias grow in most light conditions, including artificial light. Allow the soil to dry between waterings from early spring to late fall, and water in winter just enough to prevent wilting. Do not feed during the first 6 months or in the winter. Feed every 3 months the rest of the year. Plant in potting soil.

SCHEFFLERA: See **BRASSAIA**

SCINDAPSUS: The most common types are devil's ivy, golden pothos, and silver pothos. These vines are usually grown in hanging containers. They do best in bright indirect sunlight, but can be grown under artificial lights. They prefer warmer temperatures. Keep the soil barely moist at all times. Do not feed during the first 6 months, and then feed every 3 months. Propagate at any time from stem cuttings.

SCREW PINE: See **PANDANUS**

SEDUM: More commonly called burro's tail, this succulent plant grows thick clusters of 1-inch leaves on trailing stems that grow up to 2 feet long. The leaves are delicate and are easily knocked off the plant. Burro's tails do best with at least 4 hours of direct sunlight a day, but can be grown under 12 hours or more of artificial light daily. Allow the soil to dry between waterings from spring to fall, and water enough in winter to prevent wilting. Do not feed during the first 6 months or in the winter. Feed 3 times a year, in early spring, late spring, and late summer. Plant in a mixture of equal parts potting soil and sand.

SENECIO: Also known as parlor ivy or German ivy, these plants have 2-to-4-inch leaves resembling English ivy. They can be grown in a hanging container or trained to grow on a stake or trellis. Parlor ivies do best in bright indirect sunlight, but can be grown under artificial lights. Keep the soil barely moist. Do not feed during the first 4 months, and then feed every other month with a diluted commercial fertilizer. Plant in a mixture of equal parts loam, peat moss, and sand. Pinch back the tips of longer stems to encourage bushy growth. Propagate at any time from pinched-back tips.

SENTRY PALM: See **HOWEA**

SETCREASEA: Also known as purple heart, these plants have 5-to-7-inch purple leaves on 7-inch stems. They do best with at least 4 hours of direct sunlight a day, but can be grown under artificial lights. Allow the soil to dry between waterings. Do not feed during the first 4 months, and then feed every other month. Plant in potting soil. Propagate at any time from stem cuttings.

SILK OAK TREE: See **GREVILLEA**

SILVER BRACT: See **PACHYPHYTUM**

SILVER DOLLAR PLANT: See **CRASSULA**

SILVER POTHOS: See **SCINDAPSUS**

SNAKE PLANT: See **SANSEVIERIA**

SNOWBALL PINCUSHION: See **MAMMILLARIA**

SPIDER PLANT: See **CHLOROPHYTUM**

SPIRAL FLAG: See **COSTUS**

SQUIRREL'S FOOT FERN: See **DAVALLIA**

STAGHORN FERN: See **PLATYCERIUM**

STEPLADDER PLANT: See **COSTUS**

SWEDISH IVY: See **PLECTRANTHUS**

SWEET BAY: See **LAURUS**

SWORD FERN: See **NEPHROLEPIS**

TETRAPANAX: Also known as the rice-paper plant, this plant grows up to 5 feet high with fan-shaped leaves up to a foot across. The white tissue in its stems is used in making rice paper. It does best with at least 4 hours of direct sunlight a day, and prefers cool nights. Keep the soil barely moist at all times. Do not feed new plants until the first spring, and then feed twice a year in early spring and early summer. Plant in a mixture of equal parts loam, peat moss, and sand. Propagate at any time from the suckers that grow around the base of the plant.

TEXAS PRIVET: See **LINGUSTRUM**

THATCH-LEAF PALM: See **HOWEA**

TOLMIEA: Also known as the piggy-back plant, it grows up to 8 inches high and a foot across. It does best in bright indirect sunlight and prefers very cool nights. Keep the soil moist at all times. Do not feed during the first 4 months, and then feed every other month.

TRADESCANTIA: More commonly called wandering Jew, these are creeping plants with 1-to-3-inch leaves. They are usually grown in hanging containers. They do best in bright indirect sunlight and can be grown under artificial lights. Allow the soil to dry between waterings.

Do not feed during the first 4 months, and then feed every other month with a diluted commercial fertilizer. Plant in a mixture of equal parts loam, peat moss, and sand. Propagate at any time from stem cuttings.

TREE FERN: See **CYATHEA**

TREE IVY: See **FATSHEDERA**

TUFTED FISHTAIL PALM: See **CARYOTA**

UMBRELLA PLANT: See **CYPERUS**

WANDERING JEW: See **TRADESCANTIA**

WINTER CREEPER: See **EUONYMUS**